Books By Rise' Harrington with Bryan Jameison

Reincarnation - *The Four Factors -*
Soul Freedom **Vol 1**

Repelling Demons
The Loving Way to Heal Ourselves and Our World
Soul Freedom **Vol 2**

Entity Attachment Removal - *Self-Help Procedure -*
The ABC of Releasing Spirit Attachments for Do It
Yourselfers -Soul Freedom **Vol 3**

Entity Attachment Removal - Manual for Mediums
and Teachers - The Secrets of Identification and
Treatment Revealed - *Soul Freedom* **Vol 4**

Guide Lights -

Attune to Your Angels and Spirit Guides
*Begin To Heal Your Life and
Move Toward Your Soul Purpose*

Publisher: Rise' Harrington

By Rise' Harrington and Co-Author Bryan Jameison,
Regression Therapist 1933-2002

http://guidelights.org
Publisher # A21QAJB759TYZR

By Rise' Harrington 1953 –

ISBN: 978-0615700717

Rev 6.07 ~ 06/26/2023

Front Cover Photo and design by Rise' Harrington

Other Previous Titles:
*Spiritual Self Mastery
Angels Are Speaking to You - How Can You Tell?
Connecting to the Angels Made Simple*

Note to reader: This book is intended as an informational guide. The remedies, approaches and techniques described herein are meant to supplement, and not to be a substitute for, professional medical/psychological care or treatment. They should not be used to diagnose or treat a serious ailment without prior consultation with a qualified health care professional.

I thank my editor Chiwah Carol Slater who so beautifully reshaped the manuscript of my original title *'Guide Lights – Attune to Your Angels and Spirit Guides'* into eloquent prose.

~ Acknowledgement ~

To God and the many beloved ones who helped shape me for my highest good; My mother Patty Harrington, Terryann (soul sister supreme), my first spiritual mentor Madge Vanhorn, the brightest cheerleader Marina Gregory and lifetime soul brother Joseph Birdsong. Most of all, I express endless gratitude to my beloved Monadic soul family, Andrameda along with Idahohl-Adameus, who guided and inspired my words throughout the writing of this book. I dearly love you all ♥

~ I dedicate this book to Idahohl-Adameus (St. Germain) and all the Ascended Masters who have graced the earth with their teachings of love, healing, wisdom and Self-Mastery ~

Introduction

Guide Lights helps all humans make a spiritual connection to their Angels and Spirit Guides, with or without religion, to heal their lives and move towards their soul's purpose. I cover many aspects of metaphysical/spiritual principles in only enough depth to inform the reader about the basics of the subject and to begin walking a path of spiritual self-mastery. My goal is to provide a primer of sorts and to inform readers well enough to enable them to move forward in an area that warrants further individual study and discipline. Pay attention to what interests you. It is your instinctive radar that will lead you to an area of needed growth or development. And if you find something that frightens you in the least, it's an absolute treasure for your soul's growth. Move toward it!

Awakening to the Divine Spirit within us is a simple process of intention and loving allowance. I invite you to open your heart and mind to allow the Light of Spirit to enter into every aspect of your life, starting *now*. As we open communication channels to our soul, our higher self and our spiritual guidance, we walk a path of richer meaning and begin to experience the loving, synchronistic, rhythmic flow of Divine Spirit in all of life.

Guide Lights -

Attune to Your Angels and Spirit Guides

Table of Contents

Prelude

My Story - Entity Attachments

My bed began shaking at night when I was 14. Someone or something was trying to get my attention at an early age. The first time it occurred, it frightened me so badly that I ran to my mothers' bedroom and told her what was happening. She brought me to my sister's room and put me in her bed for the night. Shortly after mom left my sister tugged at me and whispered loudly, "Rise' I feel it! I feel the bed shaking!!" That validation was comforting; I was not crazy or alone.

The bed shaking went on for decades but never seemed threatening. I came to understand much later in life that the cause of the shaking was from a supportive, ancestor spirit attempting to let me know that I was different. This paranormal activity was a gentle but bizarre hint that my life would be extraordinarily *different* at times.

When I was 21, I experienced a serious assault of attempted Demonic possession. What does this mean? I was physically attacked in bed by what felt and envisioned like a black panther digging its claws deeply into my shoulders and thighs. My whole body had been taken over. I was frozen in panic and unable to move a muscle. I was barely able to breathe or think but knew with certainty that if I could not at least move a muscle I would lose my life. I had to, at least, move a finger, regain command! Help me!!!!! I screamed silently. I had no voice. I used every ounce of will I had within me to exert power of movement in my body. And then, finally, my baby finger moved a fraction and feeling came back into my body. Oh my God, I was freed from it! Or so I thought.

I have learned there are Dark Forces that often use serious tactics to thwart the progress of up-and-coming Light Workers. One who was marked at birth to be a Shaman might especially pose a threat to the darker elements of the universe. Doctors reported x-rays showing an extra bone in my back since childhood. Until my mid 50's, when I read *Shamanism for Beginners* by James Endredy, I was unaware that the extra bone was one of the signs of a Shaman. When I discovered this and my guidance confirmed it, my whole life started to make sense.

This first serious brush with the Dark Forces was an important signpost in my life. It made me stronger in the long run and determined the spiritual healing course my life would eventually follow.

I learned decades later that the evil entity attacked when I was 21 was actually a Demon and one of the Demons' entity attachments was an extraterrestrial soul that split off during the failed demon attack and attached himself to me. My divine guidance protected me from a full demon attachment so that I would one day be able to write about it and to help others become rescued from Demon attachments. (The subject of Elohim Angels and Demon entity attachments is discussed in *Repelling Demons - The Loving Way to Heal Ourselves and Our World - Soul Freedom Vol 2.*)

The dark ET attachment came with an implant which acted as a GPS locator or magnet that allowed the main Demon to keep an eye on me over the years. Dark entity attacks continued infrequently for many years but were conducted by less destructive forces than the first episode. I was in my 40's the next and last time I experienced the paralyzing affect when I was physically attacked. This was the same Demon that attacked me 20 years earlier. I became fighting mad and was left feeling afraid and confounded. I somehow knew this was the last and final battle. I was done and would play victim no more.

As a highly sensitive person I was also more *susceptible* to feeling dark spirit energy invasions. Sensitive auras are soft and easier to interface with in terms of haunting. The extreme sensitivity I've experienced throughout my life has been the most challenging aspect of my nature in trying to adapt to this world. There has never been a time when I haven't felt different from everyone else and protective of my sensitivities; to sound (loud noise), to vibration (negative), eyes (to light intensity), skin (tenderness), food (allergies). Loud or sharp sounds are the most abrasive to my sensitive nature. Ambulances and loud rock n roll music send shock waves through my body that can cause temporary physical dysfunction.

In addition, there were other odd aspects to my personal psychology that caused me to feel different from others. At times, as I look back, I remember feeling like I was witnessing my life instead of living it. There was a time I recall sitting at a stop sign one morning on the way to work being suddenly aware that I was witnessing myself sitting there, like a separate conscious awareness of some kind. "What does this mean," I wondered?

Another time, I had a stream of dreams that were like flashback remembrances. Each of these dreams were familiar to me but I knew that they were not my own. This was such a significant occurrence that I chose not to forget. The stream of dreams from origins unknown, yet familiar, were given to me for a reason and I knew it would be revealed to me one day. I saved this journal entry in a file that I was able to refer back to years later when I needed it.

All throughout my teen years and adulthood I had unreasonable fears and phobias that made no sense to me. I had no reference to them in my personal life experience. I had a very confused idea about who I was personally, where my thoughts and feelings came from and in what direction I should be headed. Some of these are normal human growing processes but mine were exacerbated by entity influences clinging to my souls body contributing to my dreams, memories and emotions that I could not discover fully until decades later.

All of these influences were like roadblocks and made adaptation to life, social skills and relationships a constant challenge. Living in my head was confusing and frightening throughout the decades, but I learned to be a competent **actress** and behaved sanely most of the time, at least at work. I hid behind a long-term alcohol problem that served to soften the continual blow to my sensitivities and to avoid facing problems. I was full of self-doubt and afraid of intimacy in relationships because I had no idea who I truly was. I was so afraid of having my psychology found out that I couldn't even face myself!

No one that I knew of had such crazy problems. I couldn't talk to anyone - what kind of doctor or psychologist do you go to for help with possession attempts, shaking beds, confused identity and sensitivity dysfunction? I felt that any professional would have wanted to medicate and/or institutionalize me.

And I became suicidal. Not considering actual methods, but serious thoughts of wanting to die, very serious depression. In hindsight, I imagine my ET attachment was happy to suggest, feed on and encourage the suicidal emotion until I got fed up and started climbing out of my hole.

While I avoided traditional doctors, I did come to accept the fact that I needed help. I realized that many, if not most, of the dark force attacks were enabled by my weakened vibrations or negative attitude. It wasn't until my late 30's that I began to accept that I needed psychological help and began serious study of self-help therapies and metaphysics. It was going to take a lot of work and some years but at least I was headed in the right direction.

In the meantime, I worked and plodded on. I had created a long-term corporate career that was one of planning and controlling inventories and production lines. This was work that was inharmonious to my creative nature but gave me a feeling of control over some part of my life. It was the only part of my life where I felt I had *any* control. But it was high pressure, stressful work that stifled my artistic nature and made me extremely unhappy over the long haul.

At the start of 1999, I was at a low point in my life and was at home extremely ill with the flu. I was lying on the living room couch feeling sicker than I had in years. I just couldn't live my life this way anymore and had reached the point of soul sickness. As I lay there I just gave up and completely surrendered to the higher forces I was learning about. A swirling purple light began floating through my body and inner vision filling me with waves of loving peace. I had a knowing that this was Divine Spirit loving me, tending softly to me, consoling me. My eyes filled with tears, I was so moved by the overwhelming love. *And I knew it was time.*

Following this realization my best friend invited me to Sedona, Az for a couple of days to see his art exhibit. Being a serious hobby artist myself, this was an ideal opening to fuel and inspire my soul. I met several people that had given up regular careers of some sort to embrace the lifestyle of the full-time artist. I was very impressed and thrown into emotional turmoil. I had not painted in years. What was I doing with my life?

Sedona was the healing energy catalyst that caused me to begin spiritually expanding at an enormous rate. One month later I cashed out my 401(k), quit my 20-year soul suffocating career and went on a spiritual sabbatical. Eight months later I made my one and only trip to Egypt which further accelerated my spiritual growth in amazing new soul shifting ways.

*See cautionary note at the end this writing.

The sabbatical lasted a couple of years in which I did nothing but meditate, read self-help spiritual books and channel my Angels, Spirit Guides and Ascended Masters. I also began training with my guidance team to work with the lost soul/earthbound spirit population, to counsel and help them cross over to the spirit realms.

The next ten years of my life were devoted to my mental, emotional and spiritual healing. I started working a low stress blue-collar job that enabled me to start writing in my off time. This resulted in the creation of my first book: *Guide Lights - Attune to Your Angels and Spirit Guides*.

I was in my mid-50s when I seemingly stumbled upon the idea of lost soul entity attachments and the confusing negative affects they cause to human beings. It is no wonder to me that I was confused all of my life about who I was and why I felt the way I did. I was sharing my body and my brain with eight other soul personalities!

In addition to the dark ET soul, one was a woman with five attachments of her own and one was a warrior that attached to me in the womb prior to my birth. (Birth Attachments are a significant topic covered in *Reincarnation - The Four Factors - Soul Freedom Vol 1 -*). All of these attachments had become dormant within me because of the amount of light that I now carried but they needed to be removed and released to the Spirit Realms in order for all of our souls to progress spiritually on our own. After releasing my own attachments, I began my research into the subject of entity attachment and possession. Over time, with experience and training from my guidance team, I developed a process for helping others in the prevention, recognition and release of their own attachments. This enabled me to create my next book *Entity Attachment Removal - Soul Freedom Vol 3*.

Today my Mediumship service in relation to Entity attachments and possessions is primarily focused on providing Diagnostic Readings, spiritual mentoring, removal of soul intrusive attachments and referrals for treatment.

*I want to add a *cautionary note* here; I would not recommend anyone follow in my sabbatical footsteps. My actions of leaving a steady career to follow the call of Spirit have not resulted in the ideally sought after, personal rewards of public acclaim and financial wealth. My path has been one of great sacrifice and resulted in a very humble lifestyle. The only rewards I have received thus far are spiritual in nature. They provide me with an enormous amount of soul fulfillment and love of my Creator's Kingdom of Light and Love; that of the Earth and Above.

Amen

1

Angels and Spirit Guides - An Overview

Have you ever seen white, blue or violet orbs of light or perhaps an electric flash of light that suddenly appeared out of thin air? Or you've sensed an uplifting wave of tenderness carried on a soft breeze? Maybe you've momentarily smelled a very strong flower scent where there were no flowers present or seen a waft of smoke appear and disappear in an instant. Have you ever heard softly faint music that no one else could hear? Did you imagine it to be an Angel choir?

If none of the above examples sounds familiar to you, don't be discouraged. I believe that we all have been nudged by Divine Spirit in one way or another. The signals are so extraordinary and short-lived we usually discard these fleeting episodes as figments of our imagination. They are ignored or forgotten by most of us.

All of the mentioned apparitions are signs of Angelic and Spirit Guide presence intended for us personally. They're meant to intrigue, inspire and get our attention, nudging us to expand our awareness to a broader reality. Yes, your Divine spirit helpers are real, and they are waiting for you to acknowledge them so they can begin actively participating in your daily activities and your life journey.

We each have a Guardian Angel and a Purpose Angel. Our Guardian Angels are with us for eternity and our Purpose Angels are with us for our life on earth to help us fulfill our soul's purpose. In addition to the two Angels, we are assigned at least one Divine Spirit Guide that is changeable throughout our lifetime. These can be somewhat enlightened ancestors or Ascended Masters assigned to us specifically.

*Note you may find other authors tell you that there are more rigid or greater standards of how many angels, ancestors, spirit guides, masters we each have. Depending on our own soul's purpose and when it is that we are born on earth, our circumstances may vary to the standards of others. The important factor is what we experience and what works for the effectiveness of our lives and our own hearts knowing.

** Note: Whenever we use the word of SPIRIT further in this book we will always mean the Divine unless otherwise noted.

ANGELS are Miracle Workers, Magicians and Nurturers of the Heart.

Angels are the most radiant and highest vibrating beings in God's creation, and they are the purest expression of God/Goddess's love. They are like their hands and voice: loving messengers assigned to us 7/24 to help orchestrate the big and small miracles in our lives *especially when we ask for help.*

ANGELS are masters of:

* Love * Protection * Healing * Inspiration * Creativity

We must ask for their assistance and involvement in our lives. Because the laws of "free will" dictate our right to make all choices for ourselves Angels can only intervene on our behalf if we ask them for help. (The exception to this rule is that they will intervene to save our life if we are confronted by death before our time).

Angels love to be called on for assistance in all matters - it is their *purpose* for being. Blessing us with loving assistance is their means of evolvement. We actually deprive them of fully expressing their purpose when we exclude them from our lives. Angels *love* to assist us through our struggles and to share our joy as our requests and desires are fulfilled. It is also the Angels, more so than Spirit Guides that provide us with our dream symbols and messages. And they are the ones that help create the synchronistic events that delight and charm us. Angels cause us to look up at the clock to capture special number sequences such as three and four of a kind (if we're into numerology) and to open books randomly at very meaningful passages.

Angels can help us with *every* aspect of our lives. Ask for their assistance with; healing for yourself and loved ones, personal and professional inspiration, or guidance with a special venture you're starting. You can request them to assist you with passing tests, cooking a delicious meal and finding a perfect gift for a loved one. Ask them for guidance and help with any of the major *and* minor challenges in your life. Remember that it is their purpose and their joy to help you. Allow yourself to accept their active participation in your life. It's free, it's easy and it's an incredible blessing!

SPIRIT GUIDES are Masterful Professors of human life. They provide similar services and teachings as the Ascended Masters that have lived on earth such as Jesus, Buddha, Krishna and Sai Baba. Although these are Ascended Masters there are so many other spirit guides that are lesser evolved. A lesser evolved Spirit Guide that did not achieve Ascended Mastery while on earth is still evolving towards mastery in the spirit realms. Their guidance is just as valid to us as the master's as long as they are serving in Divine light.

How can we tell the difference between a Spirit Guide and an Ascended Master? To most of us this is transparent. What is important is to be sure your guidance system is working towards Divine light and love. Any person that **sincerely** desires to walk the path of mastery and Ascension will receive guidance directly from the Ascended Masters.

Can we feel a difference in energy between the Angels, Spirit Guides and Masters? This will certainly vary between each of us. All guidance should be treated reverently and equally. In my experience:

- ANGELS are very ethereal, soft and loving.
- SPIRIT GUIDES are a stronger energy but can be angelically soft at times.
- ASCENDED MASTERS wield a great powerful energy at times but can also feel as soft as Angels at other times.

How can we tell if a Spirit Entity acting as Guidance is serving Divine light or not?

Pay good attention to how the Spirit *feels* and how the message *feels* in your gut, (solar plexus). Does it feel right, like an intuitive hit? Does it feel good and loving? Or does it feel suspicious and questionable? (Self-doubt is also normal. You will learn to conquer this over time).

Example: Imposter guidance will provide questionable advice and often lead the human to be suspicious or confused. Something will not feel quite right. The Guides' presence will not feel loving although it might not feel dark. Neutral is not okay. It often disguises the darkest of dark. If the advice and the presence of the entity does not feel **loving**, it must be turned away.

NOTE: These false guidance entities will not be able to approach you if you invite only DIVINE LIGHT guidance to communicate with you. This is universal law! Make the word Divine your constant companion as you move forward on this path. This subject is covered in greater depth in the next chapter.

Spirit Guides, whether or not ascended, are our personal enlightened masters who guide us in the areas of life that help us to evolve spiritually and move us closer to fulfilling our soul's purpose.

Your guides resonate to your soul purpose and are specialized in the area in which you most need to accomplish growth in at this time. At certain points in your life the primary guide will temporarily step aside to enable a different guide to provide assistance in an area of his/her particular expertise. Your main guide resumes counsel once this special need has been fulfilled. This swap out of guides may be transparent to you. I am extraordinarily sensitive so I always experienced the shifts or changeouts that my guidance presence made.

There may be periods when you feel a lack of connection to your spirit counsel. This may occur when you need some time for assimilation and independence. Trust that your Spirit Guide is there in the wings ready to resume active guidance when it is determined that you're ready.

When you are shifting to a new Spirit Guide you may also feel a guide vacancy. As we progress spiritually, we graduate, in a sense, to new guides. This is wonderful feedback from the universe. The change of guides is a very positive sign of our achievement and that of our previous guide. It is a feather in their cap as well as our own. As with the Angels, our Spirit Guides evolve by assisting us to grow spiritually. It is their service to us as well as to our Creator.

Spirit Guides are like professors of universal law and spiritual evolvement for the school of earth. They possess the knowledge and wisdom necessary to guide us on our path towards ultimate soul enlightenment. Spirit Guides lead us to experiences of growth that enable us to overcome many things including:

* Pride * Selfishness * Fear * Attachment * Addictions * False Beliefs *

~ o ~

Ultimately our Angels direct us towards unconditional love, communion with our Creator and fulfillment of our life purpose. Our Spirit Guides are not meant to answer all of our questions but to steer us to the answers within ourselves. They help us to get in touch with our own inner wisdom, which is the connection to our higher, all-knowing self. Many spiritual teachings call this "the still small voice within." This is the divine spark of God within us that leads us to accesses the truth deep inside of our hearts center. That is where all of the universal truths and wisdom resides. The *heart center* is at one with God and is our most important source of divine guidance.

Many people gravitate to either Angels _or_ Spirit Guides as their primary source of guidance. It doesn't matter which we choose to start with – we each should do what *feels* right for us individually. I began with Spirit Guides/Ascended Masters because they first approached me in a powerful way that got my attention. Eventually, I became educated about Angels and have greatly benefited from working with them as well as Spirit Guides. They are wonderfully effective teammates working on our behalf.

Not everyone will gravitate to having alliances with Spirit Guides. The notion may be perceived as too 'far out there'. The topic of Angels is widespread and is supported by religions around the world. This book might be considered more of a *"new age thing"* and can be off-putting to people who have no understanding of Guides existence or purpose. I believe that Spirit Guides have always existed alongside Angels and have most often been mistaken as Angels. When we ask for Angel assistance our Spirit Guides are also authorized to assist us, whether or not we accept the reality of their existence. Beings in Spirit work together on our behalf and most of us will not know where our divine assistance comes from at any given time.

Angels and Spirit Guides will <u>always</u> assist us with our requests if it is for our highest good <u>and</u> the highest good of everyone concerned. An unfulfilled request is a signal that what we have asked for is not for the highest good – we may be headed in the wrong direction or not yet ready for what we have requested. It may also be a matter of timing and the window of opportunity just hasn't opened yet. We must learn to trust that God's messengers are doing everything they can to assist us to achieve what is needed right now and in the unfolding future.

Our friends in spirit will discourage our adoration and over-dependence on their advice. Angels and Spirit Guides are in service only to empower us and to strengthen our abilities to create wonderfully for ourselves. Idolizing them and becoming overly reliant on their guidance dis-empowers us. When we show signs of overdependence our guides may remove themselves from our energy field so that we're forced to go it alone for a while. They are still watchful and caring but we won't sense their presence. The intended result of this causes us to become self-reliant again and strengthens our own spiritual muscles. When they return to us our bond is renewed with love and appreciation.

2

Protection and Divination

Have you ever had a negative or scary experience with a Quija board?

When my sister and I were teenagers, we would place our hands on the Quija board and ask for "spirit beings" to join us and answer our questions. Our few sessions with the Quija were unenlightened, disappointing and sometimes creepy. It's very common for mischievous and confused energies to participate in Quija dialog if a non-specific invitation has been sent out. Our intent should always be to invite the highest levels of counsel to interface with us so we can proceed confidently and without interference. I do not recommend the Quija board to anyone for use.

Energies that dwell on the lower realms of Spirit may interfere with our efforts to gain guidance ONLY if we are unprotected and do not clearly state our intention to invite only *DIVINE GUIDANCE*. To save yourself from the aggravation and confusion of interfacing with lower energy beings, place emphasis on the practice of protection as you learn to communicate with the realms of Spirit.

Protection

Three methods of protection are highly effective. I recommend using all of them simultaneously to give you the assurance you need to proceed confidently and safely. Before attempting communications with Spirit for guidance, divination or meditative assistance, do the following:

First: Ask the Angels for protection. No special procedure is needed. Your requests will always be heard. All that is required is your faith and belief in this protection.

Second: Visualize your body surrounded by white light. An effective image is an elongated white eggshell surrounding your body. Use whatever imagery feels right to you as long as the image is white.

Last: State silently or aloud that you intend to interface only with *Divine Beings* of Light.

This is an example of what I use personally in my mediumship work; "I ask the Angels to protect me all throughout this day and night in Divine Light." As I say this prayer, I envision a huge sphere of brilliant white light surrounding my body far outside my physical being. Adding our visualizations strengthens all of our prayers with our own individual will and power.

Asking for Angelic protection is helpful in many areas of our lives. Ask for protection for yourself, your car and passengers whenever you drive. You can ask for protection for anything and everything, including buildings, events, and people. When you feel the presence of negative vibrations in any situation, asking for protection will help you remain unaffected by the negative thoughts, energy and behaviors of others. A shield of white light will also protect your energy from being depleted when you're in the presence of an overly taxing, draining co-worker, stranger, friend or loved one. You may still feel uncomfortable in their presence, but your energy field won't be drained.

For those that are extremely sensitive, such as empaths we recommend visualizing yourselves surrounded head to toe by silver armor. This protects your aura from sensing the negativity and overbearing energies that would otherwise destabilize you. When I do this, I ask the Angels to help fortify the armor in place as long as necessary.

Call for protection when you or loved ones are traveling, flying, or having any kind of new adventure to ensure a safe outcome. Protection is one of the greatest gifts our Angels can provide us with – *just for the asking!*

Don't let the simplicity of these methods fool you. They are completely effective!

Pendulum

** **Warning:** Some readers that are of low vibration will have uncertain results using a pendulum. Readers that are unable to hold sufficient light vibrations will not easily succeed with the pendulum. The reason for this is a user's darker vibrations will draw low or dark energy to them through the Law of Attraction (LOA). Dark forces in spirit are notorious liars and can cause great confusion. It is of paramount importance that the user believes in the protective shields and believes in Divine guidance. Proceed with caution and use protective forces before picking up a pendulum. Renew your protection often when you are uncertain.

Using the Pendulum

Pendulums are tools of divination (intuitive perception confirmation). They are one way to receive yes and no answers from Spirit to gain clarity or confirm a direction of thought or action. *They should be used only to determine the yes and no answers to your intuitive interpretations pertaining to your own life.

A pendulum can be as simple as a 1) ring or button tied to a piece of string or 2) a precious stone or crystal affixed to the end of a chain. 3) A necklace with an amulet on a chain is also a good pendulum and is ready-made in most of the female Readers jewelry boxes. Stones, crystals and metals are clearer conductors of energy, allowing the responses from Spirit to be more fluid and strongly demonstrated. (A string and a button are fine for describing introductory tools but are not effective pendulums for ongoing use). I find a 6 inch free swinging chain length is ideal for a pendulum swing.

*If you are going into mediumship or other spiritual service work then the pendulum can be used to help determine the intuitive impressions you get on behalf of a client. The client has given permission for you to read for them so using the pendulum on their behalf is ethical. It should not be used on behalf of others if permission has not been given. To do so might cause the users intuitive gifts to be minimized, blocked or placed on hold by one's own Divine guidance team. I have witnessed this occur in others that I've mentored.

Orientation exercise:

1) Protection: Ask the Angels for protection, visualize yourself surrounded by white light, and state that you intend to interface only with Divine Beings of Spirit.

2) Hold the pendulum in your predominant hand by the thumb and index finger or whatever is most comfortable for you.

3) Ask a question from guidance to which <u>you know the answer</u>. This is to determine the direction of your pendulum swing to a "Yes" response.

Example: We're pretty sure the sun is going to rise tomorrow morning. Ask your guidance if the sun will rise again tomorrow. The direction of the pendulum swing indicates the "Yes" response to your question. It will consistently be your "Yes" response. A swing in the opposite direction is your "No" response. (A pendulum that swings from left to right is my "No" response. If it swings forward and back it is a "Yes" response. Yours may be the opposite of this. Don't compare the direction of your swings with that of others.)

As you gain experience using the pendulum you may get other responses from the pendulum including:

<u>No movement</u>: No movement may mean the following:

You need to rephrase the question so it can be answered with a clear "Yes" or "No".

Your motives for asking this particular question may need to be re-evaluated.

You're not ready to know the answer.

You've asked an irrelevant question.

Moves in circular motion:
You're very close to formulating the right conceptual question. Rethink it and ask again.
Is it too complex of a question to be answered by a simple yes/no pendulum swing?

*Note: At times the response from Spirit through the pendulum may be accompanied by a strong feeling of force enveloping your hand and arm. Do not be frightened by this – it only means that your guide wants to demonstrate his/her presence. This should be a positive and reassuring sign. If you are concerned or feel fear, then renew your protection before proceeding.

Learn the name of your Spirit Guide or Guardian Angel:

The pendulum is an invaluable tool for clarifying the messages we receive from Spirit. It enables us to be confident that our interpretation is correct.
Example: When we want to know the name of our Spirit Guide or Angel, we follow these steps:

Protection: Ask the Angels for protection, visualize yourself surrounded by white light, and state that you intend to interface only with Divine beings of Spirit.

1) Hold the pendulum in your predominant hand by the thumb and index finger.

2) Silently or aloud, ask for the presence of your Spirit Guide to be with you.

3) Confirm that your guide is present by asking for confirmation with the pendulum. Proceed when you receive a confirming response of "Yes."

4) Ask your guide to communicate his/her name.

5) Close your eyes to enhance your intuitive receptiveness. It is easier to focus on internal perceptions and impressions when you tune out the outside world.

6) Now listen with intuitive ears, inner eyes and mind. Wait for impressions: thoughts, feelings, pictures or sounds. Each person will experience guidance through the senses differently. I usually don't see pictures but I receive impressions of images. There is no right or wrong way to receive intuitive information. There is only your way.

As you receive impressions, use your pendulum to clarify the message. This may mean checking each letter of the name. Often, Spirit will provide names that are familiar to us or word clues that rhyme. For example, you may perceive the words hill, air, ion and confirm that these indicate a "sounds like" name. With further intuiting and use of the pendulum you arrive at the name of one of your

Spirit Guides, Hilarion. (My first Ascended Master guide was Hilarion).

The name may come from bizarre or unexpected sources.

Example: Let's say that every time you ask for your Spirit Guide's name you hear a plane going overhead outside. On further confirmation you learn that the guides name is Lane.

When you discover the name of your Angel or guide it may seem familiar or have special meaning to you. I once did a reading for a man who was very moved when he learned his Angel's name. He had always been drawn to the name of a Disney movie character and now understood that was because the connection he'd felt for so long for the character was his Angel's name.

Caution: I would like to include a warning about becoming too reliant on a pendulum. It is not a fortune telling tool and will not confirm accurately the path in life you should choose, whether you should marry Bob or Peter or quit your job. Spirit *will* confirm whether you're heading in the right direction and guide you to make wise decisions for your highest good. Your Spirit Guides and Angels will not interfere with your free will choice by telling you what decisions to make. They know that you need to go through life's processes to learn from the results of your own choices. They will try to warn you intuitively about making a wrong decision, but they *will* allow you to make the wrong choice. Learning from our mistakes is an invaluable learning process in our spiritual growth.

Use this tool to confirm your intuitive insights as you open the doors to the world of Spirit. There will be many opportunities for exploring and expanding your understandings of Spirit as your natural instincts and psychic abilities grow stronger. The pendulum will confirm your suspicions and hunches as you gain experience of the spiritual nature of your world. Example: "Did that flash of brilliant white light represent the presence of an Angel?" Your pendulum will swing an enthusiastic, "yes"!

Is Your Pendulum Misinforming You?

The following tip is gained from user contributions and common blunders we all experience. If you suspect you have received a wrong answer from your pendulum, ask yourself these questions:

Did you first protect yourself, then determine the 'yes' and 'no' swing directions of the pendulum? If yes, what kind of question did you ask? Remember that you can only receive answers that have a distinct YES or NO response. A question about the future or a problem that may or may not be resolved to your liking is not a good question to ask a pendulum. Your Spirit Guides will not interfere with your free will to make choices and decisions that may affect the outcome of your future. You can only expect good and accurate responses from your pendulum by asking questions that, 1) verify your intuition or, 2) that serve your highest good. 'Will I win the lottery' will receive no movement or twirling in circles as a response.

Examples of questions I would use:

For my highest good:

As a writer I might ask, "Have I used the best terminology to explain the concept?"

I'm going into a situation that I feel might be challenging or potentially stressful for me. I could ask: "Will oatmeal be the best breakfast to digest calmly within me this morning?"

If you are uncertain of the best service for you to use ask; "Is this teacher, Doctor, mechanic going to serve my highest good for such and such particular need?" *I have never been steered wrong with this one.*

To verify my intuition:

I had a dream about many bananas being laid out before me one after the other. I asked, "Should I add more bananas to my diet?" Answer: *"Yes!"*

~ . ~

Before winding up this discussion I would like to emphasize another important **caution.** There is a common trap that all of us can quite naturally fall into. This is the "All Knowing" or the "Chosen One" trap. Suddenly, at my fingertips, I believe I have access to the source of all Divine knowledge. We may think, *'This is a really big responsibility and I must be* very *special to have Angels and Spirit Guides talking to me and answering my questions!'*

We need to supervise ourselves to make sure that we're not just hearing what we want to hear because it will make us feel good, wise or powerful. We will have plenty of opportunities to feel elated as guidance confirms that we are on the right track towards fulfilling our own Divine soul purposes. But that positive feedback from the Divine may take some time. Our egos may interfere and desire to have more glory in the moment. We may feel inclined to attempt healings, predict the future and advise others on insights to improve their lives.

Please be careful as this is most often the ego out of control! Our Spirit guidance will allow us to trip and even fall in order to learn the lesson of taming the ego. This may be painful and is very often an embarrassing lesson in humility. Check your motivations carefully before sharing your newfound tool and its' perceived gifts. Remember that the main purpose of the pendulum is as a tool to confirm your own intuitive insights, suspicions and hunches as you explore the spiritual nature of your world as it pertains to _your life_ and not to that of others. Please use it responsibly.

NOTE: Our Spirit Guides have been human in the distant past and still have a sense of humor. They will at times misinform us to teach us a lesson in response to a frivolous question. At times they may not respond at all. This is how we learn what kinds of questions we should and should not ask our friends in spirit.

3

Intuition - Recognizing Spiritual Guidance

All of us have psychic senses. There are no exceptions to this. These senses have become largely dormant in most of us through centuries of neglect, denial, and suppression by religious authorities and society. Intuition, however, has survived intact over the millennia as is demonstrated by the newborn baby reaching for the mother's breast instinctively. Intuition is the natural instinctive power that enables us to develop communication and interaction with Spirit.

At some point in our lives we have all experienced an intuitive nudge, a gut feeling or hint of some kind from the natural guidance system within us. When we open communication channels with Spirit, our intuitive senses naturally become activated and begin to develop more fully. We should anticipate an increase in extrasensory perception and start learning what our senses are telling us.

When we ask our Angels and Spirit Guides for assistance, we need to begin listening, sensing and watching for signs of guidance. The responses from Spirit can be extremely obvious or very subtle.

Obvious signs leave no room for doubt. They come as clear, direct responses to our requests or as warning signals. Example: Many, if not most, of us have acted on very powerful urges that have saved us from serious accidents or disasters of some kind. In those moments, we responded blindly to very strong, natural, intuitive urges, also known as instinct. My mother modeled this response for me at a young age.

When I was a kid, we sometimes went to the large flea market in San Jose as a fun weekend family outing. On one of these weekends, as we were getting ready for our flea market adventure, my mother said that something didn't feel right and that we shouldn't go. My father thought her feelings were ridiculous and insisted on going anyway. We piled into the car, my father at the wheel and it refused to start at the turn of the key. After several of my father's attempts to start the car, my mother burst into tears and said we were *not* going – something was very, very wrong. We stayed home that day, and on the evening news we learned that a major accident on the freeway had caused a tragic multiple-car pileup with many serious injuries. This was the route we would have taken, at the same time of day the accident occurred. My mother's intuitive voice saved us from being part of this tragedy and made a positive, lasting impression on my young mind. The car started up just fine the next day signaling protective Angel intervention had been at play.

The above example illustrates an obvious intuitive message of warning from Spirit. The less obvious and more frequent communications from Spirit are the *subtle* signs received by our intuitive senses. Subtle signs are vague and need some interpretation by our reasoning minds. But we need to be careful in the reasoning process, because Spirit guidance is rarely *if ever* logical. Trying to make logical sense of signals from Spirit only causes confusion, and we can lose out on the intended message entirely.
Example: A less obvious sign of intuitive guidance might be a subtle urge to make a turn in the direction opposite from where you were intending to go. Following the *"feels right"* impulse of the moment can save you the aggravation of being stuck in traffic or facing some other regrettable problem.

One day years ago I had intended to shop for groceries in the small downtown area where I lived, but I felt an impulse to drive an alternate route. Since the impulse made no logical sense, I ignored it and continued in the direction I was headed. Sure enough, as I got closer to town, I was stopped in traffic by a long Flag Day parade. This wasn't a huge aggravation but sitting ten minutes stuck in traffic was a non-productive delay I could easily have avoided.

Logic-based training becomes ingrained in us at an early age. It's not easy to convince ourselves that following our intuition is a better way to live in this world when most of our intuitive nudges don't seem to make sense. Doubts will surface now and then as we learn to work with our psychic senses. Doubts are overcome as we experience the positive and negative results of following or denying our intuitive instincts. The tug-of-war lesson of logic vs. intuitive *feeling* is best learned through the trial-and-error method, which seems to be the only way to fully convince ourselves that intuitive guidance works. When we choose not to follow our instincts, we face the painful experience of learning why we should have!

I am not encouraging you to ignore your intellect. I am suggesting that you will become more greatly empowered when you consider your *feeling senses* in addition to your intellect. This will enable you to live your optimal and most fulfilling experience of life. Ideally it is best to *feel* first and then to consider intellectual review in light of our feeling.

~ o ~

Our intuitive instincts are our means of receiving and interpreting communications from Spirit. When we ask for guidance, our questions and prayers might be answered in many different ways.

Common signs of guidance:
~Dream messages: Dreams provide a wealth of guidance to assist us with our daily challenges. Pay attention to your dreams!

~Sparks of white light. These are always a sign of encouragement from your Angels. Their way of saying, "right on!"

~Sparks of blues, pink and green as well as other colors may come to you indicating Spirit Guides and elementals are present as signs of encouragement.

- *Color key: Any color of the rainbow indicates positive beings of light/love. Darker colors of grey and black indicate the opposite.

~Suddenly, a thought comes into your mind or profoundly wise words come out of your mouth in conversation. You know it's not like anything you would normally come up with. (Spirit sometimes spontaneously channels messages through us.)

~You overhear a stranger offering a suggestion to his or her companion and you instantly recognize that it's an answer to your own question/problem.

~You have a sudden urge to switch on the TV to a particular channel. The program is about something you've been studying or wondering about and shines a new light on the subject.

~Suddenly you hear soft or loud knocking on your walls or ceiling. Don't panic! This seems to be a common experience for many of us that are working with the Angels. Unless the Angels are delivering a message of some urgency the knocking will generally be soft. In the event you hear knocking you should conduct a pendulum Q and A session to determine the message the Angels are attempting to communicate. Was the knocking in relation to what you were just thinking? Something you just read or heard?

~You feel compelled to open a book at random. There, on that very page, is the answer to something you've been puzzling over or an insight you needed.

~A book falls over by invisible means as you browse through the bookstore shelves. Pick it up and check it out!

I was searching for spiritual inspiration in a bookstore one day. As I browsed the Self-Help section, I heard a book fall on its side on a nearby shelf. I picked the book up, looked it over, and decided I wasn't interested. I replaced it upright on the shelf and continued browsing elsewhere. When the book fell on its side two more times, I knew it was a message that guidance was determined to get my attention. I bought the book and later discovered the healing gift it carried for me.

I've listed only a few examples of the ways in which Spirit communicates with us. You will experience many signals and communications that are unique to you. It is helpful to start a journal of intuitive experiences, signs of guidance and coincidences (synchronistic events). Writing down our experiences is a means of digesting and accepting our experiences and helps to ground us in our new earthly spiritual reality. We can look back at what happened in the last week or so and see intuitive patterns developing.

Whether the intuitive pulls are major or minor, it is always our inner guidance system steering us to the right places at the right times to seize the best possible outcomes and growth opportunities. In this way our lives are enhanced, and our prayers are answered.

Exercises: Intuition Practices

Our natural sensory gifts of intuition are the subtle forms of guidance that nudge us daily. These subtler forms require greater attunement and practice to utilize effectively. By attunement I mean that we need to pay attention and be watchful of our senses and impressions in addition to our normal intellectual thought processes throughout our day. Our intuitive senses should play a much larger role in our lives and we can strengthen these senses by exercising them regularly.

The following two exercises are offered to strengthen your intuitive skills. Both are fun ways of learning and are extremely effective.

Parking with the Angels

Ask the Angels to lead you to the most ideal parking places when venturing out in your car. You can simply ask for the best or specify your needs: a shady spot, the one closest to the store entrance, the safest place, etc. After you've made your request you have only to follow the intuitive nudges you receive when entering the parking lot. You may have to pause momentarily and feel the subtle nuances. It will feel right to turn one way or another or to go in a different direction than you normally would. In just moments you should find your ideal parking place. Once you start this practice, you won't stop. As long as you follow your intuitive feelings, it works every time!

Some of us will probably feel silly or bothersome asking for Angelic assistance at such a mundane level. That's okay – just try it. You'll soon be convinced that it's a gift and a very natural part of our human experience, if we choose to use it.

Remember that the Angel's purpose is to enhance our lives in *every* way. The parking exercise is a very simple way to begin interfacing with Angels in our daily activities. It is a low-stress, easy-to-manifest and gratifying means of affirming our belief in Angelic assistance. And it demonstrates their ability and *willingness* to participate in our lives, even at the mediocre levels of our experience. By enlisting our Angels in our ordinary activities, we allow the mediocre to be transformed into spiritual activities. This begins to expand our awareness of Spirit in all of life and makes life itself more meaningful.

Shopping with the Angels

Angels are the best of all shopping companions. Ask the Angels for assistance in finding the best bargains, lowest gas prices and most complimentary products from your shopping excursions. The Angels are more than willing to help. Make your request known before you arrive at the store and enjoy your adventure. Don't be surprised if you suddenly feel you should go to a store you don't normally visit. Pay attention if a fruit or vegetable suddenly looks vividly good to you; your body needs its nutrients and you're receiving intuitive guidance to buy it. You may feel an urge to go down an aisle you rarely frequent. Do it - you'll be guided to something you really need, or you'll finally find the right gift for that loved one who's so hard to buy for.

I don't always find what I've asked for the same day, especially if my request is very much out of the ordinary. It can take a while for specialty items to manifest, so I ask in advance when I need something special. My brother-in-law is hard to buy gifts for because he's built a successful business and has everything he needs. I ask for help in finding something special for him weeks in advance to allow plenty of time for potentialities to form. One year I had no ideas for my brother-in-law and asked the Angels for help in gift finding. About a week later I had a dream that I was in a store seeing a large Scrabble display. When I went to the bookstore that weekend to do my gift buying there was a center aisle display featuring various kinds of Scrabble. This was the sign - I knew the Angels were at work here. I also knew my brother-in-law didn't need or want a Scrabble game but there must be something else there for him. Sure enough, on the same table I found a game board based on his favorite HBO series. As he opened and unwrapped it the gift became a fun conversation topic at the family gathering. The Angels scored again.

Shopping with the Angels will spark your life with light and magic in more ways than can be described here. Our lives are so enriched by their ability to turn the ordinary into a lovely adventure of anticipation, gratitude and sometimes amazement. Truly, there is no end to the gifts of abundance and delightful surprises our Creator's messengers can provide, all for our highest good. Shopping with the Angels gives us the experience of reaping that wealth regularly. As our experience grows, so does our *faith* and *trust* in our Creator and Spirit companions.

Giving thanks comes naturally to most of us, but I would like to place an emphasis on showing appreciation when working with the Angels. To strengthen your bonds and grow closer to them, always remember to express heartfelt gratitude for your Angel companions and their gifts. Each time you recognize a request fulfilled, holler a silent "thank you!" to your Angels. They will feel your expressions of loving appreciation and feel fulfilled in their purpose.

4

Raise Your Light Level - Get in the Flow

Vibration is the emanation of consciousness (as energy) in varying degrees of light or dark. How we think, eat and behave is impressed upon the personal energy that we radiate. If we were measured, as an average, most of us would range in vibration between varying shades of grayish colors - not light or dark, but somewhere in between.

Raising the vibrations of our physical, mental and emotional self is necessary to achieve and maintain a strong connection to Spirit Guidance. When our vibrations are raised, we emanate lighter energy, and the gap between physical and spiritual dimensions is lessened. This makes our communications with the higher realms much easier and the depth of our experiences richer.

It is necessary to practice a lifestyle of light and positive attitude in order to grow spiritually in our relationship with God's messengers. Development of this lifestyle is accomplished in the same way we learn any other skill or discipline. There are ups, downs, and periods of progress in between. No matter how hard we study, we will sometimes fail tests, feel down in the dumps, and even lose faith once in a while.

As we experience the ups and downs of the spiritual initiate we can, at times, feel lost and disconnected. Our prayers seem to go out into an empty void. When we're in a negative or depressed place mentally and emotionally, our communications are actually dimmed. The heaviness of our vibrations weakens our connection to Spirit Guidance and disables us from being able to sense the loving attention of our Angels and Spirit Guides. We are also prevented from receiving or recognizing the answers from Spirit to our requests for guidance. <u>A barrier has been erected between realms to protect the light from our darkness</u>. We are the unwitting creators of this barrier.

When we are vibrating at a high frequency, we feel uplifted, at peace and inspired. We've all experienced this feeling at times in our lives when we've been moved by a beautiful piece of music, an inspiring film or a new romantic love. These times of upliftment and soaring of the heart are usually short-lived, but at least for moments they inspire feelings of peace, love and happiness that fuel our souls. We are temporarily awakened to the underlying and all-pervasive presence of God's loving genius in the world.

~ o ~

In the beginning we were formed into being from the light of our Creator. Over time we became lost to the light, and we have lived through the ages in semi-darkness. There are many theories about how and why we lost the connection to our light heritage. At this point we don't need to explore the reasons we became disconnected, but we do need to reawaken to the light within us so that it can once again illuminate our lives!

So, how do we reclaim our light? We can learn to create a framework of intention that sets us up to experience moments of magic and wonder in our lives much more frequently. This concept embraces the principle of positive thinking at its very best. The intent is to create feelings of peace, love and joy without waiting for life to bless us with seemingly random experiences of divine inspiration. We can create these desired feelings by reprogramming our thoughts and choosing a lifestyle dedicated to living in the light.

Here is an example of positive intention and mindset:

~I intend to think positively – *no matter what.*
~I look to see the positive in all things. If I am unable to see it now, I have faith that I'll eventually

see the aspects of good in all my experiences.
Perhaps there's a lesson to be learned.

~I am willing to be open, receptive, and tolerant of
others. I release all criticism and judgment. There is
something lovable in *everyone*.

~I practice an attitude of patience and forgiveness.

~I do not let fearful thinking rule any of my
moments. I place my fears in God's hands and
release them for the highest outcome to unfold.

~ Faith, trust and hope are my guiding forces - I have
faith in the processes of life.

~I am grateful for all the blessings in my life. I
understand that a focus of gratitude creates a
continued abundance of blessings in every aspect of
my life.

~I let love be my guiding force always including
times of trouble and uncertainty.

*Tag this chapter with a marker so you can return
frequently for thought pattern changing reminders!

~ o ~

As we practice positive thinking and loving
behaviors, we begin to experience the flow. This is
the force of God's spirit flowing through all of life on
a much higher vibrational scale than we're used to
living in. The flow is divine love-light in motion,
moving forward, intertwining all of us in the one

spiritual flow, arranging divine expression for the highest good of all.

The flow is a very natural part of life and is very accessible to all of us. Sometimes the flow just happens to us like a magically timed interlude in our life plan. When we're very spiritually evolved and/or truly love our work, we're in the flow quite naturally much of the time. Love is the very essence of light, and when we embrace it as our mode of operation, Spirit draws all of the things we need into our lives like a magnet.

For those still floundering in the semi-darkness, these interludes of flow seldom occur. Most of the time, we have to make a clear choice to practice being in the light to get ourselves into the flow. Practicing reprograms our thinking into new, more positive ways of being.

With practice we become more and more accustomed to being in a lighter space with extended periods of inner peace and feelings of contentment. The greater the determination in our practice, the easier it gets.

Self-Mastery ~ God's Toilet

Walking this path consciously is making the choice to take responsibility for Mastery of self in creation of our lives and futures. Choosing to manage the thoughts I entertain in my mind enables me to be a person of Self-Mastery.

It is not easy. Many of us have been subjected to negativity and difficult circumstance for much, if not, all of our lives. If it has been constant, by the time we're young adults it's very ingrained in us. We continue to carry the worst of our families and society in our consciousness, the brain storing the programs and the patterns that have been running repetitive tapes within us all our lives. (Reference below picture). Self-pity, fear, old stories, self-criticism, revenge, curses, hate, old patterns, doubt, judgment etc.

Some may say, "Well, I can't help what goes through my mind!"

Who can? Do you think your creator God but these programs and patterns into place? Certainly not. Your life experience has programmed your subconscious mind through your circumstance and your reaction to it. You have used your own God-given free will choice to accept, reject, fear, retaliate, become victimized, run away from etc.

This happened to me repetitively. Bummer. He says, she says. It happens. They always do. I can't stop it.

I can't help it. What the heck am I supposed to do about it?

Release it down God's Divine Receptacle and flush it.

God will take your mental trash and recycle it into Divine Light.

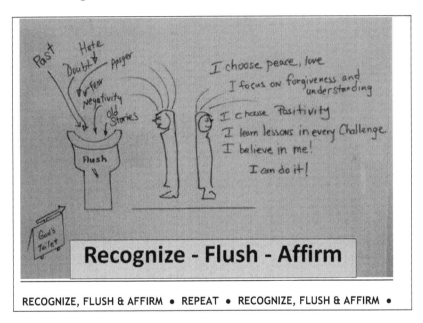

Recognize - Flush - Affirm

RECOGNIZE, FLUSH & AFFIRM • REPEAT • RECOGNIZE, FLUSH & AFFIRM •

So, once you recognize a negative thought pattern, imagine the divine toilet in front of you whether you are sitting, standing or walking. Imagine the thought stream flushing down the divine white, cosmic toilet. And then, replace the negative thought with an affirmative. *I forgive them, I will learn the positive lesson from that. I decide to be positive this day no matter what. All negative things have a positive truth inside. Truth can be found in every circumstance. God leads me forward into light. It is always my choice what I choose to think and feel!*

The single most important ingredient to making affirmations effective is **feeling**. Play, have fun. Act it out emotionally – feeling your desired outcome is the key to successful conscious and subconscious programming and absolutely creates your future. *Feel* successful, *feel* powerful and *feel* abundant. This puts the **Law of Attraction** to work! F*eel* fortunate, loving and loved. You truly are these things when you reprogram your brain, *change your beliefs* and *allow* yourself to be made anew.

This is the creation of Magic at its core. Visualize, Affirm and FEEL. 1 2 3 . . .

Remember the little engine that could? *I think love, I think light,* **I think I can** *choose only love and light!* I think I can, I think I can, I think I can achieve self-mastery over darkness!

Do this over and over again. Think, release, flush and then affirm a positive replacement. I still do this throughout my days when necessary. **It is my choice until I leave this earth; to purify my mind, to love myself for taking command and to be at peace.**

This is how we eventually reach a high vibrational light and love that enables us *to talk to Angels as God's messengers*. We practice over and over again, day after day after year after decade so that our vibrations are so high and loving that negativity and darkness can hardly reach us any longer. Only for moments at a time as we emotionally struggle with the downsides of life with loved ones and other earthly relations. Then we pick ourselves up and immediately get back on track affirming all things of positivity, light and love again.

It's *not* easy - but it is simple!

By practicing the simple processes designed to raise our vibrations, we are naturally uplifted into the light. Embodied within the emanation of light is the *flow*. When we're walking, talking and *being* the light, all our senses are open and flowing, transmitting and receiving, in the *flow*. This is when we experience miracles of divine synchronicity, those marvelous coincidences, lucky events, and momentous inspirations.

When we're in the *flow* we move toward the life of our greatest potential and spontaneously express our unique gifts fully attuned to the spirit in all things. We're fully living in the present moment. We are not carrying the past or future with us; we are simply in the NOW.

We've all heard the words from the Book of Proverbs, "as a man thinketh in his heart, so he is." Be on guard – your own affirmations and beliefs are creating your future! Will it be positive or negative, light or dark? It's up to you.

Does this sound overly simplified? It truly is that simple. No one else has the power to make you think a single thought. You are the sole commander of your mind and the company you keep within it. It is always your choice.

I am not suggesting that acquiring the self-discipline needed to change your mindset from negative to positive is easy. It is extraordinarily difficult for so many of us – but it is simple! *You have the opportunity to take back your power NOW.*

~ 0 ~

Regardless of new positive intentions, negative thoughts *will* continue to pass through our minds now and then. They will only get us into trouble when we choose to entertain them and build on them. Negative thinking is learned behavior. The behavioral role models provided by our family and society have ingrained in us repetitive patterns of negative thinking. After twenty, thirty, or forty years of living with negative thought patterns it *seems* almost impossible to break them.

I am still susceptible to negative thought infiltrations and have to reverse them. Something in life will trigger a negative reaction in me and I'll immediately revisit old critical thought patterns. But now, I only allow myself to entertain these thoughts long enough to recognize them. I then create a reverse positive affirmation to neutralize and release (flush) the negative thought. The point is that I refuse to entertain negative or unhappy thoughts and immediately focus my attention on something neutral or positive. And since we're being honest here, I have to admit that I am not "in the flow" as often as I'd like to be as I write this book. Sometimes being "in the flow" simply means being in non-resistance while dealing with challenging circumstances.

It's all about choice. No one has the power to make us think or feel anything. It's always our choice. We can choose to release a negative thought impulse or reaction at any moment, no matter what situation we're in. We are ultimately either in control of our thoughts or out of control in every moment, every day of our lives. Let's Fake It until we Make It!

~ Affirmations ~

Our thoughts cause us to feel emotion. Thoughts such as "I hate this, I resent that, I am always so broke" etc., stir up negative feelings within us. Negative emotions lower our vibration rate so that we become physically denser. Emotions like irritation, anger, hate, resentment and fear trigger physical symptoms within our bodies. We may experience a headache, nervousness, asthma, stomachache or high blood pressure. These are a few of the short-term symptoms negative thinking may cause. Longer-term negative thinking can create much more serious physical implications.

The good news is that the practice of positive thinking fueled by positive emotion has an immediate short-term remedying effect. It changes the energy we are expressing and the way we feel emotionally and physically in the present moment. *It can relax us, relieve headaches, restore normal breathing and lower blood pressure instantly.*

Long-term changes are achieved with continued practice. In the example of the "just my luck" person, a positive counter-affirmation repeated often enough will change the person's subconscious belief that he or she is unlucky. Example; "I am a worthy and valuable person". "I allow my abundance to grow every day in every way". This states a positive intent to alter and eventually change a negative belief. Just make sure that whatever affirmation you choose to counteract a negative belief or thought pattern is reasonable. To be effective, it needs to be something *you* can reasonably believe. Choosing to counter a thought of "I am broke" with "I am rich!" is not an effective approach. "I have everything I need in life as I need it" is a more reasonable affirmation for your conscious and subconscious mind to accept in the beginning. You can improve on the scope of your affirmations as you progress. Ask the Angels to help you create the affirmations that will work best for you – and ask for assistance in remembering to use them! Affirmations take practice and determination, but they *absolutely* do work!

Beginners on this path may find the reorientation to light-focused living quite a challenge. It takes determination and continual practice to maintain a light body, mind and spirit, especially in today's often chaotic world. It's okay to slip up. Just pick yourself up and get back on track. Do not chastise yourself for reverting to negative thought programs. If you slip up a hundred times in one day, congratulate yourself for paying attention and take corrective action 100 times. Pat yourself on the back for doing something positive to take command of your thoughts. Mental activity (thinking) is energy utilized. If we use our minds negatively, we actually *lose* energy. Positive thought is positive energy; it *energizes* us.

The more we practice light techniques and positive thinking, the longer we will be able to sustain light vibrations and feelings of inner peace. We lessen the gap between the higher and lower realms by lifting ourselves vibrationally to be more attuned with our Angels and Spirit Guides. As we learn to raise our light level, spirit guidance is more easily able to meet us halfway to assure clear connection between realms.

Another benefit to raising our light vibrations is the expanded consciousness that results over time. The intuitive or psychic gifts you already have will be magnified, and other skills will be developed quite naturally. When I first began light practices, I saw pale swirling colors and vague shapes in my inner vision. A couple of years later as my light quotient grew my intuitive gifts developed. I began to see with my inner vision the full shimmering light image of my Spirit Guide's face and sparkling eyes.

Light Practices & Rituals

*How to Raise Your Own Frequency and the Vibration of Your Space. *See also Visualizations*

All of the following methods provide an upliftment of the heart, mind and spirit, which in turn raises the light vibration of our physical bodies. These techniques have an immediate effect and can only be sustained over time only if we continue to practice and renew them.

Establish a routine, if you can, for spiritual sessions. Select a space in your home or other place of choice where you are comfortable and have privacy. This can be inside or in nature. Perform all of your spiritual practices on a regular basis in this spot to begin with and make it your own sacred space. Setting up a special or sacred space is a good way to set the mood for spiritual sessions. Cleaning and uncluttering our meditative space and home is an important way to raise the vibrations of the environment and lighten the flow of energy around us.

Choose ideas from the following list to establish your special space and adapt your own ideas or preferences.

~Create an altar of your most precious things; candles, crystals, Angels, figurines, herbs, incense. Anything that makes you feel inspired, special, close to God and the Angels will greatly enhance your experience of upliftment and communion with Spirit.
~Light candles and incense.
~Burn white sage for the purification of energy surrounding your space.
~Listen to beautiful, soothing and relaxing music.

~Create your own sacred ritual of readiness for meeting with spirit for meditation or prayer.
~Think loving thoughts or repeat love affirmations with feeling.

As we focus on loving thoughts while really feeling the meaning of the words, we are uplifted spiritually. When I initially became dedicated to spiritual practice I meditated daily for long periods of time. In meditation I often repeated these words from the Beatles song: "All you need is love - love, love, love..." over and over again. I focused on feeling love to lift myself higher and to sustain this level long enough to achieve communion with the higher realms. Do whatever it takes, even if you feel silly. You have no witness except the loving beings of guidance you are reaching for. Your Angels and guides are cheering your every effort and sending waves of love to assist you.

~Read spiritual, religious or other uplifting books regularly. When you're down in the dumps, pick up your reading material for inspiration. Have a book of this sort in progress at all times or keep your favorite on hand to reread when needed.
~Listen to spiritually oriented teachings or novels on CD while you get ready in the morning, as you drive to work, or as you wind down in the evening.
~Spend quality time communing with nature.

~Keep a tall glass of water nearby at all times as a conductor of Spirit. Water accommodates spiritual communications as it magnifies the intuitive impressions we receive from Spirit. (Test this in the shower. Close your eyes and notice if your inner vision is greater when you are in the water than not).

Breathing Exercises

Breathing exercises are key to raising our vibrations and aligning our physical and spiritual bodies as one. As we breathe in deeply while simultaneously slowing our thoughts, we are going within ourselves, deep within to the core self, the quiet simplicity of being. The simple exercise described here is widely used and highly recommended by Spirit. Follow these instructions only to the extent that you can do them *comfortably*. Do not strain yourself in any way.

Sit in an upright position in loose comfortable clothing.

Make a conscious effort to inflate your abdomen as you breathe in. This will maximize the benefit of each breath.

Breathe deeply in through your nose to an approximate count of four and hold the breath for a count of four. Exhale fully through the mouth until the abdomen is empty (approximate count of six to eight).

Repeat this breath three times:

Inhale deeply through nose (**4** count)
Hold   (**4** count)
Exhale completely through mouth (**6-8** count)

You should feel slightly exhilarated by this exercise and experience an increased sense of calm. Use this breathing technique prior to meditation, channeling, using the pendulum, performing healing and all other spiritually focused exercises.

Visualizations

Visualization is our most powerful tool of creation when accompanied by emotion. If visualization is difficult for you, like color, imagine something like an object or scene very familiar to you. Try imagining a wedding band for the gold color and a rose as pink. For silver you might imagine the tinsel on a Christmas tree and for white a snowy landscape.

Each of the following visualization exercises will serve to raise your vibrations: *(Caution: doing these exercises at night may cause sleeplessness)*

~Visualize your aura expanding and becoming a brilliant pink, white or gold. Let yourself expand and become brilliant, radiating your light in an expanded circle around you. Sit quietly for some moments basking in your own new light filled aura.

~Visualize yourself taking a shower in white, silver or gold light rays pouring down from the heavens, washing over you. Imagine you *feel* the sweet, subtle rush of light penetrating every cell of your body, *infusing you with light. Feel yourself becoming lightened.* Bask in this light often; let yourself revel in the delightful radiance.

White Heart Sun - Light Technique (Adapted from - Edith Fiore) Excerpt from "The Unquiet Dead"

"Imagine that you have a miniature sun, just like the sun in our solar system deep in your solar plexus. This sun is radiating through every atom and cell of your being. It fills you with light to the tips of your fingers, the top of your head, and the soles of your feet. It shines through you and beyond you at arm's-length in every direction - above your head, below your feet, out to the sides, creating an aura - a brilliant, dazzling, radiant White Light that

completely surrounds and protects you from any negativity or harm." End Excerpt.

The reason this exercise is so effective is that we are imagining the truth of God's living light inside of our bodies. I recommend the **heart** to be the center of this exercise as this is where our God Christ spark exists, but either the solar plexus or the heart chakra will be effective. As we fill up our bodies with this brilliant sparkling LIVING White Light you will feel God's presence within you! *And demons will run for their lives!*

*** The **White Heart Sun** is my very favorite exercise and I highly recommend this method for immediate upliftment and rejuvenation.

~Fill your workplace with the light of your choice to set a lighter tone. If you're having some difficulty at work, pink light will help to create a love vibration in the environment. Visualize pink light filling your workplace prior to going to work. The Angels will be happy to help you with this also; just ask for their assistance. This not only helps you but also benefits everyone in your workplace.

You can also project light to a future event that you plan to attend, or to any place you feel needs to be uplifted by light. I use this technique when venturing into a place I haven't visited before or a place I feel nervous about going to. The light then becomes the prevailing presence. When I arrive in an environment that I've treated with light beforehand, I feel comfortable as soon as I get there. Light is the substance of God's love. When used with high intent, it works wonders to create harmony and the highest outcome for every occasion.

Don't be concerned if you have difficulty visualizing colors or other images. When I began learning visualization techniques, I was unable to see the image I was trying to create. Instead I *pretended* I could see the image. With practice this pretend imaging began to produce results. I began to see the image through my feeling senses and inner vision. Through feeling/sensing/seeing the color, I experience it fully in the way that is natural to me. My means of doing this may be very different from others'. God has created each of us uniquely. Concentrate on the way that comes naturally to you instead of trying to match someone else's intuitive skills and abilities. In the event you can't visualize, simply pretend. It works!

Does it seem like we're just psyching ourselves out when we practice these kinds of ritualistic and imaginary exercises? YES! *That is exactly what we're doing!* The practice of imagining with feeling creates a new reality of experience for us by convincing our subconscious minds that what we imagine is real. I believe this is how God created the world; through enormous loving emotion imagining the universe and humanity into being. Creating us in his/her image, giving each of us the same qualities of imagination and emotion to co-create our lives with love, peace, joy, and abundance.

I encourage you to practice these exercises daily or as often as you can. The practice of imagining ourselves as light stirs the soul memory of our divine nature. Over time we begin to have glimpses of who we really are; the spiritual/physical *personification of God's love expressed*.

~ o ~

Over time, as we sustain living in the light, it becomes apparent that synchronistic events and things we desire are naturally drawn to us with little effort. Natural magic becomes the rule instead of the exception. The parking places are there, shopping experiences continue to be gratifying and things seem to be going consistently our way. We no longer need to ask for these things from our Angels and guides. We have expanded our relationship with the world to include our loving companions in Spirit and it has changed our lives. Our consciousness is expanded, our vibrations are higher, and we begin, quite naturally, to draw to us all the things needed to support us in life and in fulfillment of our divine purpose.

5

Meditation - Key to the Inner Realm

Meditation is the method for opening a pathway to your soul record, the cosmos and the voice of Spirit guidance. By quieting all thoughts of the ego mind, meditation allows us to bask in quiet consciousness, to be at peace and to listen within. In this inner silence we can sense our soul yearnings and the essence of our ultimate purpose. We may receive "knowing" insights and gain clarity with regard to internal dilemmas by listening to our hearts' truth. The heart is where we commune with spirit and learn how to heal our past and present soul grievances.

Meditation enables us to exercise our intuitive skills and become more confident in our psychic abilities. When our thoughts are stilled, we become open channels of pure consciousness. In the silent space of consciousness, we are open receptors to the higher perspectives of illumined guidance. We may receive intuitive insights and sometimes the inaudible communications from guidance known as telepathy. This is step one to the skill development of *Channeling Angels* for those whose vibrations are high enough.

Telepathic communication from Spirit is most often subtle, and this can cause us to doubt ourselves. We ask ourselves, "Did I make that up? Was it really guidance? How do I know?" We know when we're hearing the truth by how it resonates within the heart. Truths gleaned intuitively speak foremost to the heart and soul, not to the reasoning mind. The heart's truth is undeniable and should not be questioned based on logic or intellectual knowledge. Illumined guidance is consistently wise and loving, and *always* for our highest good.

How do we go about getting to this still place within?

Stillness is accomplished through single-minded focus, in other words, through extended focus on a single point. The point of focus can be an object, an image, a thought, loving feeling or a sound. Mental stillness through focus allows the senses to open to higher consciousness and enables the mind, body and spirit to simply *be*. Deepak Chopra explained the concept of meditation and the process of achieving a meditative state in a manner that finally made sense to me. He explained that there is a pause between each of our thoughts, especially as we switch from one subject to another. It is this pause that we want to focus on and learn to extend. The following is an example of the typical whirlwind of internal dialog common to so many of us:

"What should I fix for dinner tonight? Doesn't really matter - I'm going to get home late - let's make it simple. (Pause) The auditor is coming tomorrow - what should I wear? Be conservative. No. Well, maybe. What dress slacks do I have that are ironed? Yeah, the gray ones. (Pause) Did she mean what she said? Damn, she can be such a bitch. (Pause) She probably didn't mean it. Let it go. (Pause) Oh, man, I forgot to pick up the dry cleaning. I'm not going to have my favorite blouse to wear. Oh well, (pause) let's start that diet tonight - no time like the present. Oh, yeah, *right*. Well, maybe tomorrow." *Yackity-Yackity-Yak...*

Consider the squiggle symbol ~` to be thoughts or internal dialog and the dash - to be pauses between thought:

Thought ~`   Pause -

In meditation, our goal is to recognize the pauses between thoughts and to extend them purposefully into one long, drawn out pause (--------------------). And each time we return to a chatty thought (~`~`~`~`~`~`~`~`), we need to bring ourselves back to center and pause again (------- ~`~` --------
~`~`~`~`-- ~`~`~` --
-------------).

To quiet the mind for an extended period, choose something simple to focus on. It can be helpful to focus on a pinpoint of light in your imagination, or to concentrate on a mantra or affirmation. Many teachers say to simply focus on your breath or chant "OM" repeatedly. Any object or idea that feels right to you and enables you to focus without mind chatter will be effective. I imagine a horizontal line that extends over my inner vision. Sometimes this line becomes the horizon, where the sky meets the ocean or the land. Use something that feels good or neutral to you, something that will allow feelings of relaxation and well-being. The key is to use something so simple it will enable you to focus without any interest, thought or judgment. Simplicity is the key; the goal is to simply *be* and to observe the presence of silence within.

MEDITATION: PRACTICE SESSION

Outfit yourself in loose, comfortable clothing, such as pajamas or sweatshirt and sweatpants. You want your body to be comfortable so that physical stirrings won't distract your attention. Sit upright in a comfortable chair in a place where you can feel peaceful and become quiet. Soft music, incense and lit candles are all good mood setters for meditation, but are not necessary. Whatever feels good to you will be best.

Secure your privacy. Turn off the phone ringer and turn the volume of your answering machine down to zero. Consider earplugs if you live in a noisy neighborhood. You will fare much better if your meditation is uninterrupted by abrupt sounds.

1 - Perform your protection exercise (ref chapter #2):
Call on Angel protection and surround yourself with white light.
2 - Breath deeply (ref chapter #4)
* Inhale -4 count   * Hold-4 count   * Exhale 6-8 count.
3 - Close your eyes and begin to relax deeply.

Begin to focus on the object or mantra of your choosing. We will refer to whatever you choose to focus on as your means for coming to "center." Each time your mind entertains a thought, simply turn your attention back to center and concentrate on your point of focus. Once you have achieved stillness in your center space, simply sit in observance. Leave your senses open and just *be*. You are not happy, not sad, not assessing or judging a single thing. You are just *being* in the moment of pure consciousness.

Allow yourself ten to fifteen minutes per session to start with, and increase the time to twenty minutes or more when you're ready. Longer meditations may be needed for energy work, guided meditation practices and group exercises. Some of my own private meditations can last well over an hour. It really depends on you and what you desire to achieve through meditation.

During your early practices with meditation, your experiences may be "start and stop" with little meditative success. If you do not achieve your idea of success in the first few sessions, *don't be discouraged*. You will be able to achieve stillness for at least a few seconds. Consider this a successful start. Your willingness to do this for yourself and for your soul and spirit will be met with enormous encouragement from the higher realms.

*As you continue to practice, your guides and Angels may at times delight you with gifts of essences, colors and images to encourage and inspire you to continue meditating regularly.

Love and Imagination are key factors in successful meditation sessions. When we emanate love our vibrations are lifted, which greatly enhances our interface with Spirit. Imagination enables us to navigate and develop perception of all that we are experiencing in the inner realms. Love lifts us higher to experience the fluid, ever shifting energy of light and imagery of the higher vibrational dimensions. The *psychic eye* (mind's eye) within us can enable us to see the energy patterns of the higher realms of Spirit. Energy takes on the appearance of color and form in meditative states, and we use our feeling sense and our imagination to form perceptions of what we're experiencing. Over time, as we become more experienced meditators, the imagery becomes more consistent, and our imaginings become clarified to the point where they are of familiar form and expression. This concept will become clearer as you progress in your meditative sessions.

There may be times when you'll be astounded by the things your inner vision shows you, or you may feel physical sensations of being "out of body." In either case, there is never anything to fear when experiencing meditative adventures. *Because you will take the steps necessary to enter into meditation protected*, you will be able to trust that anything you see, feel or sense is of a Divine nature.

My sister often experienced the sensation of being sucked out of her body as if through a tunnel when she meditated. When this happened, she would abort her session because she was frightened of losing control to unknown forces. I tried to assure her that it was probably her guidance wanting to treat her to a light bath, but she hesitated for a long time to venture into deep meditation again. When she was finally ready and willing to trust in her processes, she decided to try again. Back in session, she released her fears and was lifted into what she described as a profoundly 'glorious experience of light and love' that made a "once in a lifetime" impression on her.

The only thing that will ever hold us back from progressing spiritually in our meditations is our own fear. In an instant, a fearful impulse can drive our vibrations spiraling downward and leave us sitting in the dull, drab existence of the semi-darkness or worse. But don't give up! In another instant we can insist on basking in the light and lift ourselves right back up! I've done so, what seems like hundreds of times. Our negative patterns and fear-based thoughts will be overcome with continued determination and the desire to *live* in the light of love.

Meditation is an effective tool for healing because it magnifies the core truth of all personal problematic circumstance. When we see the causes of our pain with clarity, we are able to more easily forgive others and ourselves. Once forgiveness is given, we are able to see more clearly the Divine purpose underlying all grievances as lessons for growth, and we are healed. This process is begun when we allow ourselves to address the restlessness within as it comes to our attention. We might ask ourselves, "Why am I feeling hurt, agitated, envious, etc? As we stop and listen, we receive answers revealed from within.

Your soul will reveal buried issues to you through your emotions so that they come to your attention for healing. Hurtful feelings, resentments and unforgiven events may surface once in a while during meditation. Unresolved issues from your early life and even infancy may rise within you, one at a time. This will only happen when the guidance of your Higher Self determines that you're ready to address the darkness in your past. You will then be guided through the processes of healing. Your dreams will also reflect these same issues to assist with your understanding and resolution as you heal.

~ o ~

I had some real difficulty in the beginning of my meditative practices. I was completely undisciplined, and my mind ran in circles around the clock. My progress in meditation was slow at first, and at times I just gave up. One particular day when I was rebelling against guidance's counsel to meditate longer, I received a comment telepathically: "So, do you choose to be a weenie whiney one?" That got my attention, and I'm pretty sure I laughed. I had sometimes jokingly used that term in reference to myself and others. Spirit had used my own words to motivate me, and it worked. If I wanted to be the master of my destiny, I had to get control of my mind - and the moment was *NOW*.

Mental discipline, focus and concentration are needed to achieve effective meditations.

You'll get to know yourself as you observe your patterns of repetitive thinking. Don't turn it into an internal tug of war. Having a sense of humor and patience with yourself will make this practice a lot more enjoyable. And the rewards are *great*. You'll increase your ability to focus in your relationships and in your work and personal interests because you will have tamed your mind and gained inner command, focus and centeredness. These all contribute to a greater sense of wellbeing, self-confidence and inner peace.

There are numerous resources available on the subject of meditation. Most communities offer classes for learning and practicing meditation. Local groups advertise for participants through free metaphysical publications. There are also many books written on the subject. It is possible to learn meditation without books or instruction, but it is helpful to have resources available when we feel the need for support and feedback to validate our experiences.

Each of us will experience meditation in our own unique way. It is wonderful to have a friend or group to share your experiences with, but don't be surprised if some of your sessions are beyond your ability to put into coherent words. You may choose to keep your sessions private because of the intimacy of your experience.

Always bear in mind that your inner realm is solely *your* domain. You are ruler and pioneer of each session you venture into. Don't be swayed by the expectations, measurements or claims of others. This is your solo journey, to be taken in *your way* and in your time.

Also, remember to enlist your guides and Angels to accompany you on your inner journeys. They have waited so long for your readiness! Their purpose is furthered as you begin to open the doors within yourself and to the higher realms through meditation. As you reach out with your heart and your imagination to embrace your larger family of lighted ones, they receive you in a return embrace and illuminate every step of your journey.

~ o ~

Peace and contentment can be found in life without formal meditation, especially if you are an evolved soul or have found other practices for communing with Spirit. Quiet time communing with nature, inner contemplation while listening to beautiful music, and painting a picture are examples of natural meditative activities. Some find their connection to Spirit surfing or riding a horse. If your soul is not urging you toward meditation, then choose only the practices that feel right to you. We are each at a different level of growth, and we each have a unique purpose in this lifetime. Our guidance will steer us in the directions we need to explore when we are ready. Don't ever force a discipline that doesn't feel right or necessary to you. Individual readiness is the prime consideration when starting any new spiritual practice.

6

Finding Balance and Grounding

If you have spent time practicing the lessons of the previous chapters, you may have already experienced feelings of temporary disorientation. This chapter will offer simple suggestions you can use whenever you feel unbalanced and need to regain your footing.

~ Balance ~

Common symptoms of imbalance include feelings of being out of body, spacey, or not quite all there. Most of us experience feeling unbalanced, to some degree, as we open new and exciting doors to the spiritual realms. This is especially true when we're coming out of a deep meditation session or the first time we discover a special communication from our guides or Angels. Feeling "out of it" is common and nothing to be overly concerned about. All symptoms are temporary, and there are immediate steps we can take to get back to feeling normal. Grounding our physical body and energy field (aura) to the earth is a necessary and easy skill to learn. The steps are simple as well as enjoyable.

For some of us, the etheric realms have such a draw and are such a pleasure to hang out in that retaining our footing in everyday life can be a challenge. This is especially true for very sensitive people, of which I am one. I have always gravitated more to the spiritual than the material aspects of life. Human companions of like mind and sensitivity have been scarce, and I have had only a couple of fulfilling long-term friendships in my life. It was in the realms of Spirit that I found loving acceptance, appreciation for the gifts of my nature, and understanding and encouragement for my otherworldly uniqueness. There was a time when I was on an extended work sabbatical and lived alone like a hermit. I meditated for hours and read and channeled every day. I loved the spirit realms and felt so at home there. This made it difficult for me to navigate between worlds in any sort of balanced fashion. In the end, though, I had to realize that God had made me to be on the earth and I needed to incorporate the world of Spirit into my daily life. I made a decision to serve in the world and to share what I'd learned. This is what enabled me to find the necessary balance to move forward with a goal, grounded on the earth while remaining spiritually connected. The writing of this book was very grounding.

Communing with the spiritual realms is not meant to be an escape from this world. It is meant to enhance and expand our experience of life on the planet. We are all here on the earth at this time for a reason. No matter how special, sensitive, creative, magical, or profoundly unique we may perceive ourselves to be, it is no accident that we came to be here. It is only by grounding to this world that our earthly bodies can be sustained and enable us to fulfill our spiritual purpose, our reason for being here.

I have learned that it takes *all* of us to make a whole. We all learn from each other, and each of our unique gifts is required to bring God's creation to wholeness. What if all the sensitive people on earth decided to gravitate to the same place on the planet and live together? How would the rest of the world learn sensitivity? Years ago, my sister asked me, "How come I'm always the strong one in the family? Why do *I* always have to be strong?" My sister has always been a model of strength for me, and because of her example I have over time learned strength. How could I have done that if all the really strong people in the world had moved away to the same corner of the earth?!

The point I'm making is that you are needed for your special uniqueness. If you feel like the oddball in your family or on your block - join the club! You're exactly where you're supposed to be. Share yourself and your unique gifts with everyone in your corner of the world. You are *absolutely needed here.* Accepting that truth is *very* grounding.

Some of us can feel completely out of touch with our families. It is important to say here that we are not suggesting you stay away from or in obligation to your birth families. We are suggesting only that you express yourself authentically when you are with them.

~ Grounding ~

The following are effective visualizations and other methods you can use when you feel the need for grounding. Choose the ones that resonate with you or develop your own methods that emulate the following examples.

Soil - Breathe deeply and allow yourself to imagine your bare feet standing in rich soil. Wiggle your toes and feel yourself bonding with the energy of the earth. This can, of course, be done outside in nature if your circumstance allows it.

Tree - Sit comfortably in an upright position. Breathe deeply and imagine you are standing barefoot before a large tree. See yourself spreading your arms wide, hugging the tree deeply and fondly, feeling its warmth and nurturing strength. Better still, go outside and hug a tree!

Food – Eating is a wonderfully effective method of grounding. You may have the urge to eat food that feels grounding to you. Generally, this will not be light foods like fruit, veggies or candy. Most likely, you will be drawn to hearty foods like potatoes, nuts, bread and other starches. Allow yourself to eat something hearty when you feel the need for grounding. Let your body communicate intuitively to you its need for grounding foods. You will gravitate to the foods that will best serve your needs.

*Note: Remember that this is about balance. Some mystics, psychics, and channels seem to be susceptible to a subconscious belief that they've been given free license to overeat for the purpose of grounding. While food is necessary at times for grounding purposes, overeating for extended periods is not necessary and is contrary to our goal of achieving balance.

Walk – Go for a walk outside and breathe deeply of the fresh air. An invigorating walk that exercises the body also balances your energy very nicely, especially if your surroundings provide a walk through nature.

Read – Read a book or magazine, some fiction or current events that will give you a sense of normalcy. Reading is a focused, centering method for calming the mind and bringing you back to earthly reality.

Grounding in a Shopping Mall?

I'd like to share less obvious methods of grounding that many of us might not think of. When we've been really focused on spiritual study or have come from a really high energy spiritual gathering, we can feel really high-wired to the point of being very uncomfortable.

An easy and convenient way to release high electric-type energy is to get out into a place where there are a lot of people. I and too many others tend to isolate when our symptoms are the most disturbing and this is not always the best thing for us to do. For those that do not live in secluded places, going to a shopping mall or public place with an outdoor square - anywhere that other people are gathered can be a wonderful way to exchange energies and gain grounding.

When we are so highly spiritually focused, we become overcharged and need to disperse some of the high vibrational energy with others. In turn, others who may be less spiritually inclined are excessively grounded and need uplifting. The energy exchange happens naturally as we move through places where other people are collected. You get grounded and they get lifted. No mantras, visualizations or special requests from Spirit are needed. ***This is natural magic at its' best!***

~ o ~

Friends and support groups are another good source of feedback for grounding and balancing.

Spiritual Internet websites have opened up a widespread network of light workers around the world sharing their experiences, channeling's, healing, etc. Doing an Internet search with the words "spiritual" or "metaphysical" will lead you to a vast number of websites to choose from. You can spend as much time as you want reading their material. Sign up for free newsletters and learn about online classes and worldwide meditations. You will find an assortment of spiritually focused offerings to choose from.

Whatever avenues you choose to explore as you delve into in your spiritual pursuits, remember to keep it all in balance!

7

Self-Love and Our Resistance

When I was young, I had a special affinity with nature. The wind and sky intrigued me and filled me with wonder, a magical presence was in the air and trees and a loving embrace within the breeze. Within this entrancement I felt uplifted and wonderfully alive. I would gaze up at the sky and feel *so very precious*. These were always moments when I was alone. My private times with nature sparked a belief and hope in a magical life that has sustained me throughout my life. I hoped that someday I would find the meaning of my secret belief in magic.

As I grew up and began to learn about fear, limitation and sickness, I took on the beliefs presented by the world around me. The magic that had been such an integral part of my being as a child faded over the years into a mere glimmer of hope far in the distance. I threw myself into a high-stress career that failed to complement my creative and sensitive nature; it left me feeling empty of energy for myself and the things I loved. Decades later, I came to a point in life when the ache in my soul was so profound that I was forced to make drastic changes in my life.

I entered into a long period of self-healing, using processes I found in books and various self-help methods that enabled me to reprogram my thoughts, emotional patterns, and beliefs. Changing my beliefs was the easiest part, because I had never fully bought into the beliefs of mainstream society. The hardest part was reprogramming my thoughts and overcoming old patterns of fear, defensiveness and negativity. As frustratingly painstaking as it was, I was determined not to give up. It took much longer to make real and lasting change than I would have liked, but I *finally* came to a point where I was able to love myself, and life, again. My Spirit relationships were my major source of guidance and healing; they reacquainted me with the natural magic of life I had longed to rediscover.

The magic, of course, was the Spirit inherent within me and all of existence.

My healing and renewal were made possible because I fought hard to overcome internal programs created out of false beliefs inherited from the generations before me. We live in a collective craziness, reacting to each other from a base of individual beliefs inherited from misguided people (parents) who misinform us because they don't know any better. The beliefs we adopt and call our own are the root cause of our resistance to light, love, and life itself.

Every person assesses the world and their life experiences through the filters of individual perception. Our perceptions are shaped by our beliefs and attitudes about life, based on our personal history: our family training, culture, education, relationships and experiences. If we've been taught fear-based beliefs and selfish attitudes, we'll encounter obstacles on our path toward making spiritual progress. These obstacles are largely beliefs and attitudes having to do with what we perceive to be true and real about ourselves and the circumstances of our lives.

When we're struggling against the natural flow of life, there is usually one reason for our resistance: what is being presented to us in the moment is not in agreement with what we *think* or *feel* should be happening based on our *belief-related expectations*. The more we resist, the more painful a situation becomes. Have you noticed?

In chapter 5, "Meditation," I shared my sister's concerns about feeling lifted out of her body whenever she meditated. Her expectation had been to achieve peace and serenity, as this is what meditation promises. Being treated to a higher vibrational light bath was not in her programming, and her fear posed resistance to the gift that she was being offered.

Trust, faith and allowance enable us to release our fears, judgments, and internal resistances to allow circumstances to unfold in the flow of Divine order.

I myself was plagued with feelings of unworthiness for much of my adult life. No matter how hard I prayed or how long I meditated, I didn't believe, in the depths of my being, that I was worthy of having my prayers answered. This form of resistance is sure to sabotage any effort to receive the best that life has to offer, or even to have a simple prayer fulfilled.

Spirit Guided me to practice self-forgiveness as well as forgiveness of others. I couldn't love myself and feel worthy of our Creator's gifts until I was able to forgive myself for creating such unhappiness in my life. I did a lot of work on forgiveness, with a great deal of success, but I still felt something was missing. I felt better about myself and about life in general, but self-love still eluded me. I was missing the key to self-worth.

Idahohl-Adameus (St Germain) Speaks: *"It is of paramount importance that we each know ourselves and learn to love ourselves enormously as our Creator does, indeed."*

Louise Hay promotes self-love through mirror talk. The technique is to stand in front of the mirror, meet your own eyes in the reflection, and proclaim your love to yourself. This isn't as easy as it sounds, because in order for it to be effective you have to believe the words you're saying. I was a tough nut to crack, but I was determined. I practiced and practiced mirror talk over an extended period until I finally believed. I cried in relief. The fact that I never let myself off the hook, never gave up – that I kept trying over time – demonstrated to me that I was absolutely worthy of my own love.

Listed below are three of the most common obstacles to making successful spiritual connections. Fear, doubt, and unworthiness are emotions stemming from unbalanced beliefs and experiences. Each of these need to be honestly assessed and corrected if we are to become spiritually well balanced. Once false beliefs are addressed, they must be healed in order for us to most fully embrace our spiritual nature and self-love.

Fear: It's so common to experience uncertainty and fear when confronting the unknown world of Spirit. The most prevalent fear is loss of control. In this case, we should consider the truthful perspective that all of existence is the expression of our Creator's Spirit. As we expand our awareness to encompass the spiritual aspects in all of life, we become more empowered to effect positive change in our lives. Instead of losing control, we *gain* control.

Most of us have not been well schooled in the spiritual nature of our being. Instead, we are taught to focus almost entirely on the material aspects of life. Now, as we do decide to open our minds and hearts to expanded truths about the nature of our world, we are freed to explore the infinite possibilities of nature, the universe, and life as a spiritual being in what only *seems* to be a purely material world. Our old beliefs and programs are shattered and restructured by our explorations and experiences in Spirit, proving our initial fears groundless.

Doubt: As beginners on this path, it is common to doubt the guidance we receive. When we ask for assistance, it may take moments, days or weeks to receive clear guidance in response. When it comes, we aren't sure that the words of wisdom coming into our thoughts are a message from spirit guidance or our imagination. "This isn't real," we think. "It must be my own mind, or just a coincidence that has brought this thought into my head." Trust that this concern will be short-lived. With experience and consistency, you will gain the confidence you need to act on your guidance and be certain of a positive outcome. It is not the words in this book that will convince you. It is your own experience of the heart, mind, and soul that will make a believer of you.

Unworthiness: A lot of us feel unworthy of receiving special attention from God and the Angels. This is especially true if we're carrying around guilt and regret for being far less than a perfect human being. We may, indeed, still have karma to clear and debts to pay. If we are feeling undeserving of experiencing the best that life has to offer, it is a sign that forgiveness is needed for ourselves and others.

The good news is that God, your Angels and Spirit Guides *know* you are worthy in spite of all your imperfections. Spirit knows all of our secrets and most dastardly deeds; these truly don't matter on any worthiness scale. The only thing holding us back from receiving the gift of miracles is our own feelings of unworthiness.

Feelings of unworthiness are a form of resistance; they keep all of our desires and dreams out of arms reach and prevent us from raising our vibrations high enough to receive the gifts of love and guidance coming to us from God's messengers.

~ o ~

There are countless resources and methods of therapeutic counseling available to help us work through the causes of our poor self-esteem and feelings of unworthiness. An unlimited number of self-help books, audio programs, classes and therapists are easily within reach to us all.

Louise Hay offers many tools for attaining self-love and healing the mind, body and spirit. I highly recommend her books, tapes and lectures, as well as the authors she represents.

There are many other offerings to choose from that might best suit you with your particular nature and your level of growth. Ask the Angels for guidance and you will be directed to find just what is needed to begin healing your beliefs and attitudes. *Every child of God, even the non-believer, is gifted with devoted Angels and Spirit Guides waiting in the wings for your call for help!*

Louise Hay website: www.hayhouse.com

Recommended reading: *The Power of Now* by Eckhart Tolle. Eckhart writes masterfully about resistance throughout much of this book.

8

Dream Guidance

Dreams are a natural inner resource we can draw upon almost daily as a trusted source of guidance. Dream messages are prompted by our subconscious mind, higher self, Spirit Guides and Angels. Their intent is to give us feedback to help us to get on course for our highest good. This is to move us into alignment with our soul purpose, stay on course or take corrective action.

Dream scenarios will sometimes offer cautionary messages to steer us in the right direction. They also provide inspiration and encouragement. When we ask our guidance for help, we can often find the answer in a dream message if we're paying attention. Dream guidance is free and consistent and will *always* serve your highest good. Even nightmares occur for your advancement; it may be time to look into the fears they bring up or the buried past events that are draining your energy and preventing you from moving forward.

Painful past events are something we often block or bury. These remain with us subconsciously and are stirred up in our dreams to provide opportunity for us to address them in order to heal. Unless we face our unhealed emotions we will be unable to progress further spiritually.

Not all dreams come to direct us to correct or heal life's problems. There are pleasant dreams, too – dreams that come to encourage and inspire us. A dream of a banquet or party tells us we've done well, that our spirit guidance is celebrating our efforts. A beautiful garden full of flowers indicates good growth progress on our part. To dream of a diamond is to be reminded of the multifaceted brilliance of our unique inner soul-self. To dream of birds symbolizes our inherent ability to soar spiritually, free as a bird. These are the kinds of good feedback dreams that have inspired me to keep moving forward through challenging times. My spirit friends often remind me in my sleep that I am always guided and always loved.

I consider dreams wonderful mysteries, and I enjoy the process of discovering their meaning. Some are so mysterious I am never able to figure out where they come from or what they mean in my present circumstance. I just know they have served a purpose on some level. The subconscious mind is a vast reservoir of mental, emotional and sensory input. We are not consciously aware of all of the impressions we receive from past experiences, things we've felt, movies we've seen, books we've read, and places we've visited. Any and all of these sources can influence our creative dreamscape. Know that there are some dreams that just need to be processed in your sleep, and that it's okay to just observe them and let them go. If you are meant to understand and process a mystery dream, it will return to you at another time, in a different way, to get its meaning across. Most dreams seem mysterious at first, but with a good dream book and a little soul searching you can analyze much of their meaning. I love the detective work. Much of the time, discovering the messages brought by our dreams can be fun and entertaining. It is *always* worthwhile.

There are several different kinds of dreams, the most common being those with symbolic messages. You will learn to distinguish the different types of dreams as you gain experience working with them.

Daily Event Dreams:
Meaningless, low-impact events, images and feelings from the day's experience will often fill our nighttime dreamscape. These are usually things that don't have great meaning but have made a big enough impression on some part of our psyche to warrant processing by the subconscious. Once we've processed them through the filter of dreaming, we discount and release most of these impressions without question.

Symbolic Dreams:
These are the dreams we have almost every night, the ones that seem confusing, silly or frightening to most of us. With the help of a good guidebook, the symbols and activities of these dreams begin to make perfect sense in the context of what is currently happening in our lives. You need to call on your own intuitive knowing in addition to a guidebook to get the full meaning as it applies to your life situation. Only you can ultimately know what message a dream holds for you. Example: An indication of steel might mean strength and endurance to someone experiencing a difficult time. This would be a sign from Spirit that he or she will fare well by remaining strong. Someone else, on the other hand, might receive the symbol of steel to indicate that he or she has shut down emotionally and should take corrective action.

Spirit uses symbols to instruct us in our dream world because symbols are universal and don't require language necessarily to express their meaning. As you learn to piece the dream symbols together into meaningful messages, your life and the world around you will begin to seem more purposeful and spiritual.

Example of a Symbolic Dream: The dreamer is walking along a path through a nondescript piece of land. There is thorny brush growing off to one side.

Suddenly, a monster roars from behind, running fast and looming overhead. The dreamer screams and starts running as fast as he or she can. There is a foreboding sense of being unable to run fast enough, and the dreamer is terrified of being caught. The dream ends.

Dream Interpretation: The *path* is our current direction in life, and the *thorny* brush indicates a negative attitude that is causing us discomfort. The *monster* represents a fear that needs to be addressed before it becomes all-consuming. *Running* indicates our avoidance of facing that fear. *Screams* are meant to get our attention; they indicate that this is an important message and that we should pay close attention to it *now*.

I have had many dreams similar to the one above. As scary as they can be to address, they are blessings in disguise, for they come to remind us of the need for change within. If we pay attention to our dreams and use them to make changes in our thoughts, beliefs and attitudes, we can save ourselves the pain of having to confront them out in the big, wide world. If we choose not to take corrective action, our fear will play itself out in our life experience and force us to learn the lesson the hard way!

I will use myself as an example. I blocked a serious molestation episode as a very young child. Throughout my life the Law of Attraction drew more misaligned sexual experiences into my life until I addressed and corrected the original unhealed emotion. I share this story in our chapter on Forgiveness.

To take advantage of dream messages, we need to recall them. When you go to bed at night, give yourself the suggestion that you will remember your dreams. Your stated intent is heard and registered; when you ask sincerely, your subconscious mind will accommodate your request. Ask your guidance to assist you in this as well. Angels and Spirit Guides can help make your dreams more brilliantly colorful or dramatic that will make your dreams easier to remember. They can also prompt you to wake up at key moments when the dream is still in vivid recall.

Higher Learning Dreams:
In higher learning dreams we may find ourselves in a class setting or lecture auditorium or on a campus. These are dreams that reflect the soul in lessons administered by the master teachers of the higher realms. I rarely have recall of the detail of such dreams, but I know I'm learning higher lessons for my soul's growth and spiritual evolvement. When I

wake from these dreams, I feel uplifted, as though I have accomplished something special while sleeping.

Precognitive Dreams:
The precognitive dreams play out future events. They may seem a bit more mysterious to us, as they don't appear to follow the symbolic rules of our regular dreams. When I have a dream that doesn't seem to apply to me in terms of normal dream symbolism, I set it aside to see if it plays out. I am very careful about sharing a dream that may be a future event. If the content seems harmless and it feels right to share it, go for it. If not, keep it to yourself. It was given to you for a reason, and eventually you will come to understand what it's about.

I have experienced precognitive dreams for many years. They are usually of world catastrophes, like hurricanes, tornadoes and earthquakes. Since dreams of catastrophe can also be symbolic of the emotional turmoil in our personal lives, it took time and experience for me to be able to tell the difference. In my experience, when the disaster is about a world event there is always a detached feeling void of personal connection or emotion.

When I'm given dreams of things to come, I believe there is a purpose for it: I am being enlisted to help effect change in the earth's energy in places where it is out of balance. When I'm given a precognitive dream of disaster, I perform energy healing for the region of the earth that was featured in the dream. The healing work is conducted through meditative visualization using light work techniques. Others around the world receive similar dreams or psychic messages to join in the effort to assist in the earth's healing. This positive teamwork lessens the negative effects of the predicted disaster. Visualizing blinding white light surrounding the earth lifts the vibration of the planet; when groups of people do this in concert, healing miracles occur.

Start a dream journal. Keep a tablet and pen by your bedside to use as a dream journal. Get into the habit of recording the major dream symbols as soon as you awaken. If you wait even minutes after waking, most dreams will fade away, and recalling them later can be difficult or impossible. Jotting down the major symbols immediately sets you up to come back at a later time to elaborate on the fuller dream picture.

I keep a letter-size tablet with a pen stuck to the page next to the bed so I can reach it in the dark and make key notes as I wake up in the night. I've developed a sort of Braille system; pressing down hard with a ballpoint pen, I engrave a deep line under each set of notes made through the night. If I wake up more than once, I can find the starting place for my next note by feeling the line with my fingers. I make my new notes below the impression. This allows me to record key dream symbols without opening my eyes or turning on the light. Normally, I can easily go back to sleep. If I turn on a light and sit up to make notes, I find it difficult or impossible to get back to sleep. Some people prefer to use penlights to record their dreams in bed. Most bookstores sell tools for writing in bed and recording dreams. Experiment until you find your own dream journaling style.

Review your dream notes. The plot or story of the dream is not always as relevant as the individual symbols. This is because our ego sometimes interjects story lines in an attempt to make sense of what seems like random symbolism or meaningless events in our dreams. Simplify your analysis by highlighting the obvious symbols and look up their meanings in a dream analysis book. You'll find several possible meanings listed, and if you are honest with yourself, you will receive the message you need.

Practicing dream analysis will challenge you to make changes in yourself and in your life. Dreams will guide you to identify beliefs or attitudes that are interfering with your highest expression of self. If you have fears, you'll be confronted with them. Fears that are faced and acknowledged are suddenly diminished or downgraded to what they truly are: Ignorance of the bigger picture, lack of belief in self, and distrust in the Divine order of life.

There will be times when the symbolism of your dream doesn't make sense. It doesn't seem to compute with who you are and what's going on in your life. If the symbols are strong and have a powerful impact, don't give up too easily. Meditation is a great place to search the subconscious for dream meanings. If you ask for guidance beforehand, you'll find your answer as you search within. Meditation is a safe and loving place to address your deepest issues without shame or embarrassment.

I highly recommend the dream book cited below to readers who choose to learn from dream analysis. It has been my guidebook since I began interpreting dreams over twenty years ago, and my own spiritual guidance has concurred with the interpretations offered in this book. Choose your dream guidebook carefully, as books that do not follow the universal code of spiritual symbols can be very misleading.

~ Sweet Dreams ~
Recommended reading: The Dream Book - Symbols for Self Understanding by Betty Bethards

9

Forgiveness and Healing

I believe forgiveness is a process of healing and self-liberation. The following is my personal story illustrating the self-empowerment and freedom I found through the practice of complete forgiveness.

After twenty years of metaphysical and spiritual study, I had learned enough to understand that holding onto old resentments, fears, and guilt was likely to create serious illness in my body if I didn't release them. I was determined to resolve all of the painful issues from my past, some of which were known to me, and some that were not. In this chapter I cover the most grievous one.

I carried a rage deep within me that surfaced so rarely I hardly acknowledged it. This rage overtook my emotions if I was confronted with verbally abusive or disrespectful behavior from men. If a movie included a rape scene, the rage would well up so fiercely in me that I would have to turn the TV off immediately. I wondered where this rage was coming from? It was so contrary to my easy-going nature that it frightened me.

As I progressed on my spiritual path, a continuing stream of old patterns, hurts and resentments came up to be addressed and healed. This was a wonderful time of growth for me, and my shoulders actually started to feel lighter and freer as the burdens were lifted. I began to think maybe I was done with my healing efforts, but I was in for a big surprise.

I was deep in meditation one day when the rage suddenly stirred within me. Oh lord, no way was I going there. It felt so *ugly* and dark. I didn't let myself struggle for long, though because I didn't want to run from it anymore. I had learned how freeing it was to heal the past and this was going to be a big one. I realized, if it's coming at me now, I must be ready for it. I took a few deep breaths and asked Spirit for extra guidance and protection.

At Angel urging, I reentered the meditative state and stilled my mind. From the depths of my soul, one by one, images and feelings from long ago began to surface. These pieces took form to create a traumatic experience that finally unlocked the buried memory of the molestation I suffered when I was four years old. I found my child self hiding in the closet, silently screaming for her daddy's help over and over again. No one came and no one ever knew, least of all me. Forty years later, my inner child was finally ready to pass this on to the adult to heal it and make it better.

Forgiveness didn't come easily or quickly. Many deep, soulful meditations followed. In the last healing session, I was deep in meditation when the Angels unlocked my heart. Suddenly I was overwhelmed with compassion and able to see with stark clarity the inner pain this man must have carried. He was not a happy man, and he was not liked. As I contemplated this I was filled with such compassion for the tormented soul he must have been. It was this compassionate understanding that enabled my complete forgiveness.

And with complete forgiveness the karmic wheel stopped spinning this tale, and it will not ever again occur on my soul's journey.

~ o ~

The process of forgiveness is not easy for most of us. It means we have to intentionally revisit something painful and try to make sense of it so we don't have to hurt anymore.

When we ask for help from Spirit, we are guided to resources that will help us to have greater understanding of our particular situation. When our minds are ready to open to our hearts' truth the Angels join us in full force illuminating the truth within us. We are then clearly able to see the dynamics in the relationship between ourselves and our perpetrator as they are now revealed in the light of love, and we are finally able to forgive. In this way we are set free.

We are able to forgive ourselves, as well, for our role in co-creating a painful life lesson. <u>Forgiveness of self is as important as forgiveness of others</u>. Both are necessary to completely free us from mental & emotional imbalance, physical disease and karmic indebtedness.

Now, your question might be, how did an innocent four-year-old child co-create a traumatic act of molestation? What is she to be forgiven for?

Without a belief in the Divine law of compensation or Karma it would be impossible to accept that there is a Divine purpose behind the abuse of a small child. I chose not to accept that I am a victim of life; there was purpose in this, and an opportunity for growth. I believe we are given the opportunity to balance out all of our wrong doings, whether from our lifetime on earth or a misalignment from life lived in other realms of existence. I may never understand how or why I might have committed such an abhorrent act on another but I must accept that it is fact and take responsibility for it. I can then forgive myself for past afflictions upon others, even those unknown and unremembered by me. In this, myself and the little girl I found hidden in the closet are, everlastingly free.

~ o ~

During the writing of this book, I participated in a San Diego writers' group that offered "Open Mic" nights once a month to allow us to gain experience sharing our writings in a public setting. Thirty to seventy people, depending on the season and varying factors, attended these meetings. It was an ideal training ground for me to confront my lifelong fear of public speaking.

After writing my own story of forgiveness, I knew I'd have to wait a while before I read it at a meeting. I needed time to live with the idea of sharing such an intimate personal story with people I hardly knew. I waited a few months and read other excerpts from the book until I felt ready.

When the chosen time came I rehearsed more than usual, until I felt comfortable with my delivery. Names were chosen in random order, and I was nervous as I waited to be called on to read. When my name was called I didn't hesitate to step up to the microphone, but as soon as I began reading, my body started to quake. I fought to contain a rising panic. Where was this sudden physical trauma coming from? I asked the Angels for help as I read, and succeeded in getting through the reading even though my body felt out of control. This was not a normal anxiety attack, and it confused me. I went to bed that night knowing I had meditative work to do the next day. I needed to find the underlying cause of the physical trauma I had experienced as I read that night. It wasn't an emotionally or mentally charged trauma; it was an involuntary physical reaction as I shared my personal story.

At some point in my previous spiritual studies, I had learned that our bodies retain cellular memory of all our emotionally traumatic, unhealed earthly experiences. When we're traumatized by life events, the trauma remains in our bodies unless it is addressed, emotionally expressed and healed. But I had healed my trauma through forgiveness. What remained to be done? I knew I wasn't going to be able to rationalize this. There was yet a mystery to be solved. I needed to learn from my cellular memory what imbalance still remained.

My priority that weekend was meditation. I asked Spirit and my higher self to guide me in finding the source of my remaining trauma. I stilled my mind and waited. After a while the idea of "soul retrieval" came to me. This is a term used by shamanic practitioners to name the method spiritual counselors use to guide clients to reclaim parts of themselves. These lost parts of self have become fragmented and energetically stuck as a result of past traumatic occurrences. A piece of the soul actually splits off from us and becomes trapped in the emotional energetic point (the moment) of a past tragic experience. The physical body then stores the traumatic memory within the cellular structure of the body, where it remains hidden until triggered. I asked my guidance whether it was soul retrieval that I needed to perform. The silent reply was, *"Yes."*

As I meditated on a strategy for accomplishing this, it occurred to me that I had neglected to rescue my four-year-old child self from the closet from so long ago. While I had realized symbolically that she was freed, I had yet to energetically release her from her hiding place. A fragment of my soul remained energetically stuck back there, as if suspended in time for 40 years!. Following this realization, my initial reaction to the idea of rescuing my child was distaste and shame. This little girl was so badly soiled that I felt repulsed. It's no wonder I hadn't yet arrived at peace - I was subconsciously rejecting my injured self! This sad insight was overcome within seconds as I determined to heal my past and present self, *NOW.*

Back in meditation, I revisited the image of my frightened little girl-self crouched down, hiding in the closet. I went to her as if I were a guardian

Angel, lifted her up into my arms, and hugged her for all she and I were worth. I held her and cried as I consoled her. She was so desperately in need of love, nurturing and safety. I was *so* sorry to have neglected her for so long!

Once the child and I were both consoled, I released her and imagined her hovering before me. Her back was facing me as she began gravitating backwards, slowly beginning to merge into my energy field. With an expanding swell of energy and billowy light, she integrated fully within me once again. We can now live peacefully united as one through every new chapter of my life.

~ o ~

So many of us have experienced some kind of trauma in our childhood or adult life. Perhaps you've lived through an emotionally abusive relationship that caused feelings of deep resentment. Some people have suffered violent physical abuse, and the resulting emotional and physical trauma gives rise to feelings of anger, resentment and fear. People who were belittled and/or abused as children can carry profound emotional scars their entire lives. The betrayal of friends or lovers can cause deep emotional wounds and sorrow. As adults, many of us succeed in burying the painful past and refuse to think about it. This self-deception leads us to believe we can move on with our lives without carrying the pain around with us. Some of us are so effective at burying the past that we actually forget it even happened. This, of course, only delays and prolongs our souls healing.

When we decide to embrace the light in greater degrees, we begin to experience periods of inner turmoil and upheaval. This is because most of us carry some subconscious darkness within us. Increasing light does not tolerate stagnant darkness so when we are infused with greater degrees of light, the darkness begins to stir. Unpleasant memories of unresolved experiences and relationships begin to surface. These unresolved issues may haunt our dreams repeatedly until they are addressed, or situations similar to those from our past may recur in our lives to give us an opportunity to confront them for resolution and healing. We are being given the chance to make wiser choices and to learn from the lesson offered within every painful experience or relationship.

If dark inner stirrings are not addressed, we are likely to become depressed, filled with anxiety, and sick in some part of our bodies. These issues are surfacing now because we carry enough light to be able to cope with resolving them. We have become strong enough to face our fears and demons of the past. Your Spirit Guides and Angels are with you to light the way to higher understanding and complete resolution. Facing our fears, resentments and grievances is the painful part of our growth, but it is also the way to self-empowerment and our ultimate freedom. Once we are free of fear, resentment and grief, there is no longer any need to protect ourselves from others, no reason to feel inferior, and no life challenges to be afraid of. We're now able to fully express ourselves without self-consciousness or protective shields. We're ready for unrestricted freedom of expression and interaction with all of life.

If we understand that repressed mental and emotional wounds are the cause of illness and disease, what can be done to help us heal our wounds? The remedies are always available through psychological and spiritual processes. These processes or therapies assist us in addressing and remedying the imbalances within us. As we heal the past, our burdens are quite naturally released and we experience the healing of emotions, mind, body and spirit. Ultimately, all grievances can and must be resolved in order for us to attain true inner peace and wholeness. Forgiveness needs to be a key component of any mental or emotional therapy.

~ o ~

Forgiveness is *not* condoning or agreeing with mistreatment of self or others. Forgiveness is a realization that all of existence is Love. Everything we are confronted with that doesn't look, behave or feel like love is a sign that we have a misalignment of some kind within ourselves. An imbalance offers a lesson that once learned, will bring us into harmonic balance (alignment). When we are facing a struggle with another person, there is a karmic lesson to be learned by both parties. An attitude of forgiveness expresses compassion for others, understanding that they too are learning sometimes painful lessons of growth.

Forgiveness Exercise: A review of the many different angles from which we may consider a hurtful situation can provide us with greater clarity in our efforts to forgive. Consider the method below as one guideline for attempting to understand a painful circumstance.

You may want to have writing tools at hand when you go through the following list.

1) To begin, ask Spirit to guide you in your recall of the situation or event you want to work on forgiving.

Ask for inspiration, and you just might hear the whispers of Spirit guiding you.

2) You have chosen a minor episode in your past that is still somewhat painful to think about. Ask yourself why it was or perhaps still is painful. Spend some time feeling the associated emotions and write them down. You may want to spend some time later re-evaluating this list. There is no rush; this is your process to go through in your own way and time.

3) Be *very* honest with yourself. If this process isn't at least a *little* painful, you may be hiding some truth from yourself.

4) Keeping in mind that this is a minor grievance, ask yourself the following questions:

How long ago did this happen?

How has this affected my life?

How may it have affected his/her/their life?

What does this mean to me in my present life circumstance?

What is it that I gain by holding on to this grievance?

Is it possible that I am not seeing the bigger picture that would explain why this situation occurred?

Is there a lesson for me to learn so that I can grow in understanding of myself and/or my relationships?

Is it possible that I played an active role in instigating this problem?

How would my life be changed if I forgave and released this past grievance forever?

After you've answered the above questions honestly, review the list below. These are examples of thought processes and realizations common to those who have done the work of forgiving.

1) I forgave him/her and myself for co-creating such a negative situation, and now I feel freer.
2) I shouldn't have given anyone enough power over me to hurt my feelings.
3) He/she is obviously unhappy with life and just wants company. I choose not to join in his/her misery.
4) When I really think about it, I feel sorry for him/her.
5) I'm done playing the victim. It was foolish to let my energy be sapped in that way.
6) I'm going to treat him/her respectfully, no matter what, just because it will make me feel better about myself.

Reaping the Benefits of Forgiveness:

An important step in healing life's disharmonies is recognizing the blessings earned. Blessings are the gifts received from undergoing painful experiences. We should ask ourselves, "What did I gain? What have I learned that will enhance my path? How have I grown?" The reward may be improved self-esteem, strengthened courage, or greater understanding of a spiritual truth. We may also have finally broken an age-old pattern of behavior that is *not* emotionally, physically or spiritually working to our advantage.

You may find yourself thinking similarly to some of the comments below following your forgiveness exercise:

1) The next time I run into him/her I won't have to feel awkward and pretend to be nice. I can be myself and be openly friendly.
2) I realized I was partly wrong, too. It felt good to be honest with myself.
3) It feels great not to carry a grudge anymore; it's a weight off my shoulders. I actually felt lighter after I looked at the bigger picture and forgave him/her and myself.
4) I saw that I couldn't expect others to have the same ethics, values and considerations I do. I have to accept people as they are, without expectations.
5) I'm learning lessons of tolerance, patience and love.

Minor grievances can be forgiven fairly easily if we can put our bruised egos and pride aside to revisit the past from an objective viewpoint. Whether the transgression is major or minor, forgiveness is made possible when there is a change in personal perspective from "Victim" to "Master of Self." A position of Self-Mastery is attained when we choose to take ownership of our perceptions and our responses to the world in any circumstance.

~ o ~

The above process works well for small grievances such as slight friendship betrayals, unkind acts, self-serving lies, etc. What about major issues like physical abuse, marital infidelity, rape, major business betrayal, or murder? These are tough issues to work through and may require professional help in the form of spiritual and/or psychological counseling.

To forgive minor transgressions, we can largely rely on our reasoning minds with some involvement of the heart. With major grievances, we need to put our reasoning minds off to the side and enter wholly into the domain of the heart. The heart encompasses Gods cosmic consciousness and holds all truth within it. The heart is completely illumined by the light of love. When our grievances are viewed from the center of the heart, all truth becomes accessible. We are able to see, feel and know with full certainty the truth that lay buried under the layers of our pain. This is the arena of our true light Source; God, the Angels and Spirit Guides. They enter here with us to lead us home.

~ o ~

Once you have achieved forgiveness, you can give
yourself permission to reap the rewards of freedom.
Do your shoulders feel lighter? Perhaps your heart is
singing and there's a spring in your step. Do you
want to twirl around and hug the sky?!
"Ahhh, yes, *free* at last!"

And so it is.

Recommended reading:

Radical Forgiveness - Making Room for the Miracle
by Colin C. Tipping

*Heal Your Body - The Mental Causes for Physical
Illness and the Metaphysical Way to Overcome Them*
by Louise Hay

10

Merkabah - Vehicle of Light

As I was wrapping things up with the last chapter of this book I began to wonder what else was needed. The book seemed too small at just under 100 pages, yet I didn't want to write 'fluff' just to fill more pages. I struggled for months trying to come up with a good fit for an additional chapter and finally gave up. I've learned that if I try my best and something just won't come together, I need to let it go. The universe can then rearrange the order of things so that eventually the pieces can come together, or not, just as they're supposed to.

I changed my focus completely and began to think about artistic design. The cover art had to be chosen and it needed to be something special. I knew I would never be happy with something I'd painted myself. The perfectionist in me didn't believe I could create the ultra-special blockbuster cover needed to do justice to my first book on the most important aspect of my life. So, what then should I use? I secretly wanted to play with the idea of bringing my Merkabah photos out of hiding, beautiful apparitions in the clouds that I had photographed many years ago. What an incredible showing they would make on a book cover! I asked my guidance whether I should use them for the book. The reply was clear: *"What did you think they were for?"* Wow. I had not expected that answer. Guidance had instructed me to keep them under protective cover for over a decade. I had kept these photos to myself for so many years I had lost sight of the fact that they would have a reason for coming out of the closet someday. Now, after more than 20 years of hiding, the Merkabah pictures would finally introduce themselves *and* the book!

With this realization came the inspiration for a chapter that would bring the Spirit "vehicle of light" to the attention of public awareness. I will not be able to write grandly on this subject, as the Merkabah's introduce themselves so majestically the writer in me can't begin to compete with our Creator's genius.

I am an unknown writer introducing a fairly significant subject in the overall scheme of spiritual development on planet earth. Why me? I would have thought a well-known scientist, astronaut, rock star or priest would have been able to launch public awareness of the Merkabah in a much grander arena. I have wondered why God gave such a rare gift to an unknown writer, one who was going to have to depend on a miracle to get her book published and hope for a second miracle to accomplish a lot of the marketing. The truth is that it is still a mystery, and it's supposed to be. The most I can figure out is that the voice of a common man or woman was needed to bring this light to light so that the largest percentage of the population will be able to relate to what they're reading and to the person doing the writing. If God wanted to get a message out to the masses, he'd be likely to call upon one of their own to be the messenger. It's as simple as that. The only *un*common thing publicly known about me is my name, which comes from Risë Stevens (my mom's favorite opera singer).

Although I have first hand experience, I would like to make it clear that I am not an expert on the subject of Merkabah. Most of the information presented in my book can be confirmed on the internet or in Dr. Hurtak's book discussed later in this chapter. I will clarify the use of the word to lessen the likelihood of confusion:

The Merkabah*, or* Merkaba*, is more commonly referred to as the 'Vehicle of Ascension' by spiritual organizations that teach meditation and light activation techniques with the desired outcome of ascension. Ascension is another word for enlightenment or raising of consciousness to higher planes of existence. The* Merkabah *is the light energy body that transports soul consciousness in spirit form to the higher realms.*

In line with that explanation I believe our light bodies develop naturally as we grow spiritually, regardless of our chosen path. I do not actively participate in, or conduct, Merkabah life path teachings. In this chapter I refer to the term 'Merkabah' only to represent *the presence of our Ascended Masters.*

Souls that have incarnated on earth and have developed their Merkabah light bodies through the processes of enlightenment are the Ascended Masters. Examples of widely known Ascended Masters are Jesus and Buddha among many others. Ascended Masters travel to our dimension of consciousness in their light bodies to guide and inspire us in concert with our Spirit Guides and Angels. While some people are sufficiently clairvoyant to see Ascended Masters in full body, I usually see only the Merkabah light bodies. These are five-sided (pentagon-shaped) lavender or pink energy fields of light. In this chapter they are pictured in black and white.

I frequently see Merkabah flashes of light. They usually come as signs of encouragement when I'm working in a high-vibrational mode. They seem to be saying, "Keep going girl, you're doing great!" They have been delightful life companions, providing spur-of-the-moment encouragement, upliftment and inspiration through the years of this book's development.

Now that the message of Merkabah has been delivered in the release of this book I am seeing the energy fields of my guides as well as the Merkabah vehicles of the Ascended Masters. The energy fields of Spirit Guides are beautiful round spheres of varying shades of blue & red/purple. To have my guides sparkling and flashing lights wherever I go is so endearing and makes the magic of my life real in every day. What a lovely, magical universe we reside in!

~ o ~

I believe a magic window of opportunity was opened in 1986 by the influx of light paving the way for 1987's Harmonic Convergence. This was a significant astrological event of extraordinary planetary alignments. Metaphysical and spiritual people (light workers) from around the world gathered in celebrations and meditations led by José Argüelles and others to raise the collective consciousness of the planet to elevated levels of light and a new age of peace. This influx of light raised the vibration of the planet enough to greatly magnify communications from Spirit for all of us.

I wasn't aware of this event at the time, but it occurred the same year I began experiencing stronger communications and signs from Spirit. I had begun sketching channeled drawings in bed before falling asleep and receiving brief telepathic communications from the voice of Spirit as I meditated on the drawings. The images I drew were in the shapes of mystical energy patterns. I use the word 'energy' because I felt my own physical energy field responding to the images. When I looked from one picture to another, I felt something different, often in my solar plexus, or in the form of heightened awareness. One drawing looked similar to a conch shell, another to a magical crystalline city in the sky. More often, circular spaceships were depicted.

One of the spaceships fascinated me, because it seemed extremely large and I was given a lot of detail which I embellished upon (not pictured). As I studied this drawing, I received reassuring messages of love. The drawings were in no way intended to frighten me. Instead they strengthened my trust, and I began to feel more confident when confronted with extraordinary experiences.

One day in 1986 I went to the country to visit a friend I called Gramps. Gramps was a former neighbor and adopted grandfather, and I loved him dearly. Gramps and I would share a beer outside and talk at length, mostly about fond memories of the restaurant he had owned and about his many escapades. On this day, the wind was blustery, and the clouds were performing beautifully. I felt suddenly inspired to stand up and point my camera at the sky, completely overtaken by a crazy impulse to snap picture after picture.

Two weeks later, I discovered the reason for that impulse. As I looked through the developed photographs, I noticed a strange geometric-shaped light in more than one of them. In fact, it was in several pictures, always in the same area of the sky. I was curious, and also cautious. This pink pentagon shape could have been a light reflection or technological anomaly. I didn't want to get my hopes up. Spreading the pictures out on the kitchen table in sequence, I noticed that in several photos, the shape seemed to be moving slowly behind a cloud – much as in a slow-motion sequence of movie frames – until it nearly disappeared behind it.

This was incredible. *Wow!* I thought, *what on earth do I do with this?!* I went to my spiritually adept mother, of course. Her reaction was mild by comparison to mine, but she was intrigued. She thought her friend Lavona, in northern California, might be able to shed some light on this apparition. When Mom explained to her what it looked like, Lavona said, "That sounds like the Merkabah. James Hurtak discusses the Merkabah at length in *The Book of Knowledge: The Keys of Enoch®*." Mom had this book in her personal library, and the following excerpt explained to us the purpose of Merkabah:

Excerpt from *The Book of Knowledge: The Keys of Enoch,*® chapter 3-0-1, Para 1 and 2, page 339:

1 "The souls who have reached the greatest levels of awareness and attunement with the Father are able to extend themselves through many dimensions of light in service to the many realms of specie intelligence desiring to know the meaning and direction of life."

2 "This extension throughout the various dimensional realms of intelligences is done by Merkabah."

The "souls" referred to in this key are those of our Ascended Masters. Of course, you and I are the specie intelligence desiring to know the meaning and direction in life.

Plate 16 on the facing page of Dr Hurtak's book is an illustration showing the human form inside a five-pointed star enclosed in the geometric shape of the pentagon.

Please access our website for color photograph of the Merkabah http://guidelights.org. See the 'Merkabah Explained' page of the website.

The Merkabah images from my photographs feature leading and trailing spheres. My understanding is that this indicates a group of Ascended Masters.

There will be skeptics who will doubt these pictures and my claim. I'm all right with that. My objective is to show readers what Merkabah's look like so you'll know what it is you're seeing if or when a Merkabah light vehicle visits you. Once a thing is made known, it isn't so easily dismissed as a "figment of imagination."

I see pictures of Merkabah's infrequently captured on TV, in films and in magazines, usually in beautiful nature scenes, and I always suspect that the person taking the pictures is in tune with Spirit and that his/her Ascended Master inspired the day's photo shoot. The lights will be in my life forever now, and with this sharing they'll be seen by so many more of my brothers and sisters around the world. Word of mouth and the Internet will ensure that the Merkabah and spheres of light will eventually be known worldwide.

Your Spirit Guides and the Ascended Masters are already with you. It is not an accident that you are guided to read this material. If the idea pleases you, simply request that you be enabled to see the presence of their light bodies. I first found them skyward, and now they appear to me everywhere. You may find them in a dream, in a garden or in the bathroom mirror. I would like to believe that all of us who open to the possibility will be blessed with visitations by Merkabah's and/or light spheres, the ethereal presence of our guiding Masters.

11

Spiritual Growth = Change

Spiritual growth is a process of transformation, one that is inevitable for all of us in our soul's evolution. Some of us undergo spiritual evolvement by conscious choice and others by unconscious flailing through lifetimes.

All of life is a process of one kind or another. Refocusing our intent towards a more spiritually fulfilling life is a significant path to be undergone one step at a time. There is no course that can offer "enlightenment" within a pre-determined period of time. Each of us moves forward at our own pace – sometimes soaring and sometimes dragging our feet, but always moving forward.

A natural part of the spiritual growth process is having our new understandings of reality and spirit tested by others. As you open new doors to broader understandings you will learn to be okay with your new beliefs while allowing others to hang on to theirs. The fact that we're on an enlightening and exciting spiritual path doesn't mean we're all-knowing or always right. Guard against the defensiveness and self-righteousness of your own ego. This is a pitfall in which newly budding light workers can easily get caught up in. Imagine how special you'll feel when an Angel whispers in your ear or an intuitive hunch pays off. To hear or sense the compliments and encouragement from spirit guidance is a fabulous confidence builder, and you may be told how special and unique your particular gifts are. When life seems to be going your way and magic and miracles are unfolding around you, you'll feel totally in love with your life and yourself (at least temporarily). This can cause self-centeredness and an inflated ego, which leads to a consequence I think of as an almost instantaneous karmic backlash: an inflated ego creates an imbalance within us, which in turn leads to experiences that cause us great embarrassment. While this embarrassment serves a positive purpose, knocking us off our pedestal and teaching us lessons in humility, it is anything but pleasant. I have learned this lesson well and am constantly watchful of the ego that threatens to walk the path with me.

Avoid that of playing spiritual coach. You may feel so great about your life and the new things you've learned that you'll be tempted to offer unsolicited spiritual advice to others. If not kept in check, this most often repels friends and family to some degree. A good tip to remember: If they're not asking, they may not (often won't) want to hear the guidance you're volunteering. Make sure your motives are pure when offering spiritual advice. If it is intended in love to assist another, then your motive is right on. Just be honest enough with yourself to recognize when you're offering advice with the *primary* intention of enhancing your self-image. An inflated ego does not unify; on the contrary, it creates distance and separateness.

Try to be considerate and a little cautious about who you choose to share your new spiritual experiences with. Until we are well grounded in our new belief systems and practices, we can too easily be derailed by unsupportive feedback from peers, friends and loved ones. Choose to share only with those you know will be supportive and tolerant, if not understanding. My sister is a perfect example of a supportive friend. After sharing some phenomenal (other worldly) meditative experiences I had and what I believed they meant, she said to me, "I don't believe what you believe, but I believe in *you*." I have been blessed with a wonderfully supportive sister *and* mother.

You may face resistance from friends and loved ones who cannot understand what you're experiencing. Be patient and understanding with them, as they may feel alienated by your new spiritual focus. It is you, who are changing, and the spiritual quest is a solo journey, after all. You may have a friend or two who can accompany you on your new path, but even so, your path will be unique to you. Be true to your own soul's needs even if it makes a loved one uncomfortable; just try to make considerate choices to lessen the discomfort of others. Allow your loved ones to go through their life processes at their own pace, in their own time.

If some of your friendships shift and move away from you, know that it is a natural part of the evolutionary process and that doors to new, more companionable friendships will open. The changes you undergo when allowing yourself to be true to your heart and soul are always for the best. If you are confronted with the need to part ways with a friend, ask for Angelic assistance to help you conduct your parting with purely motivated expressions of love.

Refrain from making too many dramatic changes all at once to avoid creating imbalance.
If you experience overload, confusion, disorientation, or relationship problems stemming from your new spiritual practices, you may need to take a break. A break can be fifteen minutes to focus on grounding, or it may be weeks to months of nurturing other aspects of yourself and your life. Spiritual growth is a process. Be patient with yourself, and your own internal guidance will steer you in exactly the right direction at exactly the right speed at all times.

There is no need, nor is it possible, to rush our spiritual progress. When we try to rush, we become overwhelmed, depleted and frustrated. The reason our processes can't be rushed is that processes have to be *grown* through in order to take root in our lives. We can't *be* without *becoming*. Growth takes time, and impatience breeds imbalance. We will each have a different rate of progress and our own unique experiences. It is the journey that matters, not the speed with which we arrive at each new milestone. Allow yourself to journey at *your own* pace and measure your progress against *no one else's*.

Your life will become wobbly at times. Maybe it'll just teeter, and maybe it'll turn upside down. As your interest shifts to other aspects of metaphysical and spiritual living, you'll open doors that may astound you. You can and should find supportive sources that can offer you an outlet for sharing your new experiences and revelations. This will help keep you grounded in your changing reality. Don't isolate yourself; search out like-minded people in classes, metaphysical bookstores, psychic fairs, meditation groups, and the Internet.

~ o ~

I consider myself a different person than I was at the start of my own dedicated spiritual journey. I have also changed greatly since starting the writing of this book. As I wrote the lessons for each chapter, I was forced to realize that *I* needed to master these lessons and *live them on a daily basis.* I was not consistent about walking my talk. I kept getting caught up in the everyday "real world" (I had to work in it full time, after all). I had stored away many of the wonderful spiritual lessons I had learned and was continually struggling to sustain my light level. Then, every night as I sat down to write I was reminded, to practice what I was teaching, to retrieve my spiritual tool kit and get back on track. The writing of this book was the best thing that ever happened to me! So, dear reader, thank you for giving me the motivation to practice what I preach throughout the five years it took me to write this book. I mean that very sincerely. If not for you, I might still be slumming in and out of the murky lower trenches of life.

~ * ~

~ Epilogue ~

Your life may have started changing as soon as you began reading **Guide Lights**. You opened a door that, once opened, does not close.

For me, Divine connection has allowed the merging with my higher self soul family so that the truths of the higher realms can be spoken through the collective voice that we are.

As you close this book, it is my prayer that you will be guided to loving and fulfilling adventures in Spirit as you move forward into the expression of your soul's highest purpose.

~ Amen ~

Bibliography

*Note: Books on the subjects of Spirit Release Therapy and Demons are included in the bibliography as research reference material only. I do not necessarily recommend or agree with the ideas, statements or practices presented.

Anatomy of the Spirit - The Seven Stages of Power and Healing by Caroline Myss, PhD

Arcturian Songs of the Masters of Light by Patricia Pereira

Autobiography of a Yogi by Paramahansa Yogananda

The Book of Knowledge: The Keys of Enoch® by J.J. Hurtak 1977

The Celestine Prophecy by James Redfield

Close Encounters of the Possession Kind by William J Baldwin, Ph.D.

The Complete Ascension Manual - How to Achieve Ascension in This Lifetime by Joshua David Stone, Ph.D

The Dream Book - Symbols for Self Understanding by Betty Bethards

Emissary of Light: A Vision of Peace by James F. Twyman

Energies of transformation - A Guide to the Kundalini Process by Bonnie Greenwell Ph.D.

Entity Attachment Removal - Self-Help Procedure - The ABC of Releasing Spirit Attachments for Do It Yourselfers –Soul Freedom Series Vol 3 by Rise' Harrington and Bryan Jameison

Exploring Your Past Lives (1976) by Bryan Jameison

Family of Light: Pleiadian Tales and Lessons in Living by Barbara Marciniak

A Field Guide to Demons - Theories, Fallen Angels, and Other Subversive Spirits by Carol K. Mack and Dinah Mack

Guide Lights - Attune to Your Angels and Spirit Guides - Begin to Heal Your Life and Move Towards Your Soul Purpose by Rise' Harrington

Heal Your Body – The Mental Causes for Physical Illness and the Metaphysical Way to Overcome Them by Louise Hay

Healing Lost Souls - Releasing Unwanted Spirits from Your Energy Body by William J Baldwin, PhD

The Highly Sensitive Person's Survival Guide: Essential Skills for Living Well in an Overstimulating World (Step-By-Step Guides) by Ted Zeff and Elaine N. Aron

Left To Tell - Discovering God Amidst the Rwandan Holocaust by Immaculee Ilibagiza

Love Without End - Jesus Speaks by Glenda Green

The Power of Now by Eckhart Tolle

The Ptaah Tapes: Transformation of the Species by Jani King and P'Taah

Radical Forgiveness - Making Room for the Miracle by Colin C. Tipping

Reincarnation - The Four Factors - Soul Freedom Series Vol 1 by Rise' Harrington and Bryan Jameison

Repelling Demons -The Loving Way to Heal Ourselves and Our World Soul Freedom Vol 2 by Rise' Harrington and Bryan Jameison

The Rite - The Making of an Exorcist by Matt Baglio

The Search for Past Lives (2002) by Bryan Jameison

Shamanism for Beginners by James Endredy

Siddhartha by Hermann Hesse

Songs Of Malantor: The Arcturian Star Chronicles Volume Three by Patricia L. Pereira and Sue Mann

Soul Retrieval - Mending the Fragmented Self by Sandra Ingerman

Through the Mists by Robert James Lees - British Library 1898

The Unquiet Dead - A Psychologist Treats Spirit Possession by Dr. Edith Fiore

Website: www.DivineTruth.com by AJ Miller (AJ discusses Lost Soul Entity Attachment in videos throughout his website). The term he uses for spirit attachments is "over cloaking".

You Are Psychic - The Art Of Clairvoyant Reading and Healing by Debra Lynne Katz

----- Biography -----

About the Authors

Rise' (Reese) Harrington wrote her first book, *Guide Lights - Attune to Your Angels and Spirit Guides* to document the path that she developed in response to the internal presence and attack of dark forces throughout most of her young and adult life. Her life challenges included the uphill struggle with birth and trauma entity attachments, identity confusion, childhood sexual molestation and a Demonic possession attempt. The path that she was able to develop with the assistance of her Angels and spirit guides brought resolution of her own entity attachments as she rose from the darkness into the light, steadily growing vibrationally through the years beyond reach of the dark and Demonic factors. Her written material is expanded by the shared experience of thousands of people from her readers and Mediumship practice.

Rise's extensive experience in the corporate world in the documentation of procedures has resulted in a very effective procedural style manual for self-help healing. This, her second book is the popular Entity Attachment Removal - Self-Help Procedure - The ABC of Releasing Spirit Attachments for Do It Yourselfers. The culmination of these two books makes her an effective spiritual mentor and healer for people at all levels to raise themselves vibrationally in like manner and begin to evolve into their highest expressions of soul self.

Rise' received higher metaphysical instruction and guidance from her Angels, Spirit Guides and the Ascended Masters. She has since become merged with her Monadic higher self soul group of 35 other members and is now the earth-based spokesperson of this group called Andrameda. Soul mate Dorgeck co-authors her books under his original incarnation author name, Bryan Jameison.

Rise' has practiced mediumship focused on assisting the Lost Soul population for 20+ years. In 2013 she began offering Diagnostic Readings for Lost Soul Entity Haunting, Attachment and Demonic Possession with recommended treatments. All services are listed on the website.

http://guidelights.org/servicesoffered.html□

Rise's spiritual life path has been greatly influenced by 20 years of largely career related world travels to the Far East, Europe and Egypt.

She is a professional Medium and Minister of the Universal Life Church. She was raised in Los Gatos, California and now resides in San Diego County California.

Email Contact: soulfreedomrise@gmail.com
Web: http://guidelights.org

YouTube Channel
https://www.youtube.com/user/guidelights7

Bryan Jameison

May 8, 1933 - December 2, 2002

Born and raised in Chicago in May 1933 as James S. Lewis, he worked and wrote under the pseudonym Bryan Jameison. He later had his name officially changed to the latter.

Long acclaimed as a Master Past-Life regressionist, Bryan is internationally recognized as a true pioneer in the field of past-life therapy. After creating his own non-hypnotic method of past-life regression in 1968, he went on to facilitate more than 25,000 regressions and train nearly 2,000 others to become past-life regressionists in the United States, Canada and Western Europe.